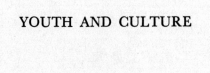

YOUTH AND CULTURE

YOUTH AND CULTURE

William Louis Poteat

The

Wake Forest College Press

1938

PRINTED IN THE UNITED STATES OF AMERICA BY
EDWARDS & BROUGHTON COMPANY, RALEIGH, N. C.

VITA

William Louis Poteat was born in Caswell County, North Carolina, on October 20, 1856. His father was James Poteat; his mother, Julia Annis McNeill Poteat. He entered Wake Forest College at the age of 16 and was graduated in the class of 1877. In 1878 he returned to his Alma Mater as a tutor, and in 1881 he was made professor of biology. In 1905 he was elected president and served in that position until his resignation in 1927. In the fall of that year he resumed his work as professor of biology and met his classes until October, 1937, when he was stricken.

On June 24, 1881, he married Emma Purefoy, of Wake Forest. A son and two daughters were born to them: Hubert McNeill, Louie, Helen Purefoy.

He was the author of a large number of articles and of five other books: *Laboratory and Pulpit* (1901), *The New Peace* (1915), *Can a Man Be a Christian Today?* (1925), *The Way of Victory* (1929), *Stop-Light* (1935). He received the degree of Litt.D. from Mercer University; the degree of LL.D. from the University of North Carolina, Duke University, Baylor University, Brown University. From November, 1936, to November, 1937, he was president of the North Carolina Baptist State Convention.

He died at his home in Wake Forest at 7:00 p.m. on March 12, 1938.

The addresses presented in this volume were selected by Dr. Poteat and are, with two exceptions, his baccalaureate addresses to the classes of 1908-1927.

PREFACE

The new world rapidly forming about us belongs of right to the young—its inheritance of dissolving traditions, the new types of freedom into which they will be recomposed, the control of the transition, the leadership of the new order. The very marks and traits of youth impose upon it these responsibilities. Its memory is too short to be preoccupied with the past. Its mind is not set, but adjustable and receptive. Its native boldness has not been disciplined by defeat. Its energy is unjaded, equal to any task. Its enthusiasms have not been cooled by experience. Its adventurous spirit is ready for any enterprise on any path into the opening future. If the path promise to be difficult, so much the better; and the tang of danger gives it fascination.

With a single exception, the addresses brought together here were made to young men just completing their college careers, pausing for an older brother's last word before springing to their tasks in the big world outside. The gifts and characteristics of youth which had enjoyed the opportunity and experience of culture called out all these discussions. The special subjects presented in them were suggested by some phase of the intellectual life of the moment, as "Patriotism" in 1916, "Kultur" in 1917, "Crisis" in 1918, "Internationalism" in 1921, "Toleration" in 1923, "Faith" in 1924.

College men and college women are alike everywhere. Lines of latitude and longitude are imaginary even in geography. They certainly count for little where the spirit of youth and the obligations of culture are concerned. Accordingly, I venture to think that what was local in Wake Forest College was typical, and that whatever word proved fit and useful there might be fit and useful wherever disciplined youth confronts its world, whether in revolt against its conventions, or sucked into its passionate trends, or confused by its changing lights, or challenged by its bewilderment and pain.

Another consideration appears to some of my friends to justify the publication of these addresses. They present the reaction of a fairly intelligent man to the changing intellectual interests of the two decades covered by them, and taken together they provide an authentic cross-section of this tumultuous and pregnant period.

W. L. P.

Wake Forest, N. C.
January 1, 1937

CONTENTS

PAGE

FRONTISPIECE.................................*Facing* 3
VITA.. 5
PREFACE... 7
THE CHRISTIAN COLLEGE IN THE MODERN WORLD....... 11
CULTURE AND HAPPINESS.............................. 23
CULTURE AND DEMOCRACY........................... 32
CULTURE AND RELIGION 38
CULTURE AND SERVICE............................... 43
CULTURE AND PUBLIC LIFE.......................... 48
CULTURE AND FREEDOM.............................. 53
CULTURE AND LEADERSHIP........................... 58
THE KNIGHT-ERRANTRY OF MEDICINE................. 66
CULTURE AND PATRIOTISM........................... 76
CULTURE AND KULTUR............................... 86
CULTURE AND CRISIS................................. 91
CULTURE AND THE UNFINISHED WAR................. 99
CULTURE AND PROGRESS 106
CULTURE AND INTERNATIONALISM 112
CULTURE AND CONSECRATION......................... 118
CULTURE AND TOLERATION.......................... 124
CULTURE AND FAITH................................. 129
CULTURE AND HORIZON.............................. 135
CULTURE AND RESTRAINT............................ 140
CULTURE AND LIFE.................................. 147

YOUTH AND CULTURE

THE CHRISTIAN COLLEGE IN THE
MODERN WORLD

Inaugural Address, December 7, 1905

To the gracious words spoken here today and many that have reached me in private ways, I am able to make no adequate response. I can now only give assurance of grateful appreciation. They impose a deep and perpetual obligation to faithfulness, and at the same time set up a standard of achievement which, though quite beyond my hope, is yet not too remote to guide and to inspire me.

The responsibility which I now formally accept I have not sought. I have loved my teaching, my microscope, and the invitation to be present at Nature's marvels under the open sky and in the deep woods hereabouts. For these obscure delights I see no compensation in the publicity of strenuous days in administration. And my poet friends who, long winter nights, have taken me up into their high fellowship—what an exchange would these be for the personal and financial problems of a large institution? There have, in truth, been moments of hesitation and recoil before this new sphere of labor. Even now these keys received from my honored predecessor grow bigger and heavier the longer I look at them. Into what halls of untried activities will they admit me? What burdens wait behind closed portals for my untrained shoulders? What doors of opportunity will they open before me? If I could be assured that, along with these keys, he passed on to me some of that wisdom which enters the right door and speaks the fitting word, and some of that cunning beneficent burglary which set flowing into the coffers of the College the wealth of friend and stranger alike; if the secret of unlocking sealed fountains of affection descended to me with these keys, I could take them up with less trembling.

There is an old Spanish maxim which warns us to beware of entering where there is a great gap to be filled. But he whose withdrawal has made this wide gap has done the work of his hands so wisely that the task of his successor is greatly lightened. Under his guidance the traditions and ideals of the College have been established in right directions. He has led it out of the wilderness and put the song of progress in its mouth. Moreover, I take comfort in the fact that the wisdom and generosity to which I am already deeply indebted are still within reach of my perplexity. I hail him today with honor and affection, and felicitate him that his name is written large on the brightest page of Wake Forest history.

Another reflection gives me heart for this new position. It is not foolish and I know you will forgive me if I recall in your presence the hope, realized today, of a father long passed into the skies. If he is pleased, I am content.

But the considerations which have mainly determined my decision are the judgment of the Trustees and the promise of a wider service of the Kingdom in the cause of education. Of the first I need not speak further. The second has suggested the topic upon which I now invite your thought—the place of the Christian College in the Modern World.

What is a Christian College?

Let me remind you that the term college was originally used of any body of associates having a common aim and work. This use is not entirely obsolete at the present time, for we still speak of the College of Cardinals and the College of Electors. But the term is now distinctively used of an incorporated institution organized for instruction in the liberal arts. In its external aspect, the college is the promoter and conservator of the liberal arts, those subjects which engage the interest of enlightened minds; it is the guardian of the culture of mankind;

it is the apparatus by which each generation is brought up into sympathetic appreciation of the total achievement of the race. In its internal aspect, a college is a body of associates in pursuit of the higher things of life, a brotherhood in which character takes form in the atmosphere of culture, in which mind comes to its own in the process of dealing with the finest products of mind—a mutual benefit society yielding dividends in efficiency and character.   Quietness and repose and openness to all the suggestions and moulding influence of external nature are best suited to this time of germination and growth.   In such a freedom from distractions and the insistent appeal of commercialism, the vision of the ideal world comes more surely and its sway is more firmly established.   For the college is at once the minister and the symbol of the supremacy of the ideal world, and the note of idealism shares with the note of fellowship the dominance of college life.

Now, in what sense may such an institution be described as Christian?   Are the liberal arts which the college cultivates Christian arts?   There were seven of them in the mediaeval scheme of education—geometry, astronomy, grammar, etc. Is the Latin syntax Christian?   Is mathematics Christian? Are the Hebrew Scriptures the textbook in the new astronomy?

It must be allowed that geometry, for example, is indeed an abstract subject.   Plato, I believe, held it to be so abstract that even to facilitate its demonstrations with material figures, was, in his opinion, derogatory to its noble nature.   It certainly has no relation to Christianity; there is no Christian geometry considered in itself.   But geometry considered as an instrument of education is quite another matter.   The highest educational thought of the time insists that the function of the teacher is the total forming of the human being, the bringing of the child into lively and harmonious relation with his whole environment, physical, intellectual, and spiritual.   Character is the teacher's crowning achievement.   If now the Christian principle is the germ and guarantee of the highest character, clearly geometry taught in a distinctly Christian atmosphere as an agency in the realizing of this Christian aim becomes as truly Christian as anything incapable of faith can be. And so of science, we may say, with Haeckel, that "it has nothing whatever to do with the subjective ideas of faith." There is no Christian science. The absurd caricature called by that name is not science, and it is hardly more Christian than the tonsured Guido, who "clipped his top hair and thus far affected Christ." But when science is laid hold of by the Christian college for the purpose of education, it becomes in the sense I have indicated Christian science. For the "climate of opinion" and sentiment is none the less positive and potent because it is unobtrusive. Indeed, the power of Christianity is never more distinct and effective than when it produces a psychological atmosphere favorable to the Christian life.

But the Christian college is not content with the creation of such an atmosphere and the results of its subtle influence, important as these are. It relies not simply upon indirection and the sweet contagion of Christian example to establish the Christian character. It uses these, but goes beyond them, supplements them with positive instruction and guidance, whose undisguised aim is to bring the student into living relation with the highest ideals in Jesus Christ.

It would hardly seem necessary to add that the Christian college is pervaded by the Christian spirit of mutual helpfulness. It will show itself in the personal relations of faculty and students. The teacher is approachable, sympathetic, generous. He is the student's best friend, thoroughly committed to his success, all round partner with him in the noble enterprise of culture. The student, on his part, cannot but be respectful and responsive. And when the association is ended the lectures may grow dim in memory and then drop out, but the lecturer never. The lessons go, but the impulse towards all noble and beautiful things remains. The moulding, cultural agency is not the teaching, but the teacher, in whom the highest demand is manhood and inspirational power. Titles count for little against personality.

I may be permitted to remark incidentally that, as regards this personal factor in education, the small college has the advantage of the large. Not necessarily, as I think, for the average number of students to each teacher need not be larger in the large college than it is in the small. Besides, special devices may be available to check the tendency in the larger institutions towards estrangement between teacher and student, as for example, the preceptorial system lately introduced at Princeton. In any case, I shall hope that the increase of our numbers here, which I confidently anticipate, with the consequent widening of our service, will not involve the loss of the cordiality of friendly intercourse between teacher and student which for these years has characterized this institution. It must not.

But in a Christian college this spirit of mutual helpfulness will show itself not less in the personal relations of the students among themselves. It demands kindness without either coddling or subserviency. It lends a hand, and with the greatest alacrity where the need is the deepest. It will hardly be denied today that hazing, no matter what form it takes, is in its essence a breach of the Christian standard. The singular momentum of the tradition which, even in the enlightened communities which colleges are taken to be, brings the practice so far down into the era of courtesy and honor in social relations, is one of the curious features of college history. The combination of cowardice and brutality in a disguised crowd to take a mean advantage of a single-handed opponent is intolerable, and the Christian standard which we maintain justifies extremest measures to make it impossible.

What I have been saying is only the application in detail of the great regulating principle of the Christian college—the supremacy of Christ. The enthusiasm of its teachers and the aspirations of its ardent youth it brings to Him. Its equipment and endowment it lays at His feet. Whatever light it has against ignorance, or guidance for life's intricate pathways, or power for social good, it submits to Him, as embracing all human need in the scope of His compassions, as controlling all life under the breadth of His law, as foretelling in the perfections of His own nature the acme of the human achievement.

The Place of the Christian College in the Modern World

Are we not met on the threshold of this inquiry by the incompatibility of the Christian college and the modern world? The modern world is a very knowing world, in high conceit with itself on the score of its knowledge; a disillusioned world, which has banished all superstition along with witches and elves and fairies. It is, besides, a free world with the pride of freedom, impatient of restraint, of moral restraint as of other forms. And it is a prosperous world, self-seeking and materialistic, with a sneer on its heavy lip at your impractical college idealism, and quite content with its crude doctrine of progress and physical comfort. Old Montaigne speaks of a certain visitor, "a pedantical gull," who yet was "a man of letters and reputation, a graduate, and wore a goodly formall long gowne." Has the Christian college a place in such a sneering world as this, such a coldly practical, emancipated world?

We need to remember that the modern world is after all the the same old world. It has its phases and moods; the mechanism and appurtenances of its life have greatly changed latterly, but its life is fundamentally the same, its needs are the same, and the conditions of all permanent and noble work in it. Again, it is the ideal forces in human history that have controlled its development. They are still supreme, in spite of our preoccupation with the earthly connections of our life. Civilization cannot permanently be "the defeat of man," as it has been called by a distinguished living critic. Moreover, religion is the germ and bond of all social aggregates of whatever grade of organization. Beyond question, all that is distinctive of Western civilization may be traced directly to that fund of altruistic feeling with which Christianity equipped it in its cradle, and it cannot now repudiate it. Once again, whatever in the past may have been true of the general aloofness of college interests and ideals, certainly today the idea of the direct and vital relation of all grades of education to the actual life which the student will lead has come to full and universal recognition.

We shall see more clearly the present place and function of the Christian college if we consider the modern world under the particular aspects of religion, culture, and the State.

Religion.—It is the less necessary to dwell here in view of the definition of the Christian college already presented. It is sufficient to remark that such an institution is a positive and tremendously effective force in the religious world, both for the individual student and for the collective work of organized Christianity. The Christian college is the safest place for a young man in the formative period of his life. In the first place, he has the picked youth of the country as his companions, choice men as regards both their social culture and their religious life. For example, eighty-eight per cent of the students in this College are church members, and allusion has already been made to the moulding and inspiring influence of reverent and capable teachers. In the second place, while life habits are forming and settling into character, the student has the advantage of regularly recurring tasks in elevated pursuits.

But what of the temptations of college life, of which one hears so much? I sympathize with that Harvard professor who, when asked to make an address on the temptations of college life, said that he would devote himself chiefly to its temptations to excellence. The temptations to evil in college are nowise different from those which assail youth everywhere; but no other community has anything to correspond with the restraining and supporting influence of the great majority of the student body. Again, it is insisted by some that the student's preoccupation with intellectual pursuits is especially un-

2

favorable to religious growth. But I venture to think that the trouble lies not in the kind, but in the fact of preoccupation, and this of course is not peculiar to the college.

But is not the tendency to skepticism especially character-istic of young men in college? I think not. It is more exact to say that it is characteristic of that stage of mental develop-ment which young men have attained when they attend col-lege. It is not wholly unlike the teething stage in infancy. Whenever the mind awakes into independent activity, as it is apt to do under the stimulus of new knowledge or a widened experience, no matter what or where the external surround-ings may be, that critical period will announce and signalize itself by putting a question mark after everything in heaven and in earth. Accordingly, we observe outside of colleges, as well as within them, this incipient skepticism, which in most cases is only a stage in the transition from a hereditary to a personal, well-grounded faith.

Of course, it is because of the wholesome developing, liber-alizing effect of the Christian college upon the individual that it becomes so important an agency for the purposes of organ-ized Christianity. The kingdom of heaven is the great uni-fying, inspiring idea of all the Christian centuries, and its com-ing realization in a regenerate social order on earth is the aim, as it will be the crown, of all our sacrifice and service. This college, as other Christian colleges, is organically bound up with this aim and hope. When the fathers laid brick to brick yonder in 1834, they did it in the assurance that they were building for the kingdom; and every brick laid here since that great day is consecrated by the same worthy and noble asso-ciation. Cut these bonds and leave Wake Forest unrelated to the purpose of our Lord to recover unto Himself the whole round world, much and long as I have loved it, I should say my farewells and seek attachment to the divine purpose else-where.

Culture.—The realm of culture embraces the provinces of

science, art, and letters. It is an important section of the modern world, and, it goes without saying, is the home of the college. Of the college, I say, but can it be said to be the home of the Christian college? Does not the culture of the time insist upon the secularization of the higher education, and so declare its own independence of religion? There is no time for discussion. I must be content with suggestion.

It will have to be admitted that during the middle decades, the last century passed rapidly from being regretfully skeptical to being arrogantly and superciliously irreligious. This was due to the unexampled extension of scientific knowledge in that period. Science seemed to be on the point of dissolving everything in its universal retort. There was nothing left to be authoritative except science itself. But towards the close of the century and on to the present time the limitations of the scientific method have become more and more manifest. Men are seeing that its triumphs concern surface problems and really leave exposed, indeed, but still untouched, the central mysteries of life and nature. "I do not know," "I do not know," is more and more forced from the lips of science, and a striking change of mien and bearing has spread over the entire intellectual life of the time. The threatened estrangement of culture and Christianity gave opportunity for closer examination of the foundations, with the result of showing their inherent affinities. Christianity has dropped the antiquated view of the world which for centuries was associated with it, and has now annexed the whole realm of culture, laying under tribute its new knowledge, the wealth of its literature, and the manifold illumination of its art to quicken the pace of the coming kingdom. And the Christian college is at home again in the world of culture.

The State.—The great task and high calling of Christianity is the salvation of organized humanity, the creation of a just society. Its method is the regeneration of the social unit. We have seen that education under Christian auspices and in accordance with Christian ideals produces the highest power and the noblest character in this same social unit. Christianity supplies motive, education supplies efficiency. Christianity gives aim and guidance, education insures leadership. We conclude, therefore, that the Christian college stands side by side with the Christian ministry as an agency for the realization of all social good.

But the Christian college has been, it must be confessed, all too slow in recognizing its social mission. For a long time it shut itself indoors from the roaring, vulgar world, and in the refined seclusion of academic shades communed with the past, quite oblivious of the problems and needs of the present. What wonder that when the last cord that binds him to his sheltering alma mater is cut, the graduate stands pale and helpless before the great, rude world where he must fight for standing room. His picture, well drawn by Montaigne in the 16th century, answers most accurately for his successors even of the nineteenth : "See but one of these our universitie men or bookish schollers returne from schoole, after he hath there spent ten or twelve years under a pedant's charge ; who so inapt for any matter? who so unfit for any companie? who so to seeke if he come into the world? all the advantage you discover in him is that his Latin and Greek have made him more sottish, more stupid, more presumptuous, than before he went from home. Whereas he should return with a mind full-fraught, he returns with a wind-puft conceit ; instead of plum-feeding the same he has only spunged it up with vanitie." And yet, in spite of this cloistral segregation, which continues, it must be admitted, even to the present in some degree, the leading men in our public life are for the most part college bred men. Not far from sixty per cent of the members of Congress are college men. That percentage will rise with the continued advance of the present tendency in colleges to a wider life. That tendency is unmistakable.

But mere collegiate training in our state and national legislatures cannot of itself purify politics and right our social wrongs. It may, indeed, but equip the forces of evil with a sharper intelligence and a higher efficiency. Culture is no safeguard against anarchy, for it does not touch the moral root out of which anarchy springs. It is a commonplace of history that some of the most intellectual periods in the career of a people have been marked by the disintegration of personality and the decay of national life. As has been remarked by one of the ablest writers on the fundamental conceptions of the State, the intellect divested of moral spirit is not a working force in the institution of righteousness, which is the condition of national life.

Here emerge the opportunity and mission of the Christian college. The Puritan projectors of the oldest educational foundation in our country aimed only at the education of the ministry, but later charters widened its purpose and proposed that it should fit persons not only for the church, but "for civil employment" as well. And so the Christian college of today is unfaithful to its calling, if it is content with fitting persons for stations in the distinctive work of the church, public or private. It must fit men for the service of the State. The mediaeval universities, from which our institutions of today are descended, were commonwealths of learning complete within themselves and, not merely in education but also in administration and police regulation, wholly independent of the civil power. Our inheritance from this system shows itself in two features of modern college life—isolation from the world of affairs and the special code of ethics for the college student. Much of this mediaeval inheritance is already dropped. The whole of it must go. The new idea found expression at the establishment in 1810 of the University of Berlin, which Frederick William III, its founder, called "the nursery of better times." It was for Prussia a weapon of war, as well as a seat of learning. And with respect to internal administration the student is coming to feel more and more that he is a member

of the civic community in which he resides and is, like every
other man, amenable to its law.   This beneficent tendency we
must carry forward to its fulfillment.   The Christian college
needs to be pervaded by an elevated patriotism.   The social,
economic, and political sciences must come more to the front.
It must multiply points of contact with the public life of the
time.   The obligations of citizenship must be enforced, and
the political career shown to be worthy of the noblest character and the brightest intellect.

So will the Christian college link itself in a new place to the
purpose of God in the redemption of society, and find a new
spring of enthusiasm in this wider struggle with moral evil for
the enthronement of righteousness in social and political institutions; and so, without actual weapons itself, move, an organizing and an inspiring presence, through the conflict and
determine its issue, like Browning's Echetlos at Marathon—

But one man kept no rank, and his sole arm plied no spear,
As a flashing came and went, and a form i' the van, the rear,
Brightened the battle up, for he blazed now there, now here.

CULTURE AND HAPPINESS

1908

A philosopher who from his old Greek grave speaks even yet in the thought of the world, described education as "friends seeking happiness together." Does your Wake Forest experience support the description? In the four years which lie next behind us regular and severe tasks have kept your growing strength at tension and set limits to the free range of the moment's impulse and preference. The like labor and restraint have marked the life of your teachers. Indeed, in the opening vistas of this occasion you are probably thinking most of the end of labor and the slackening of restraints, and you so explain not a little of the happiness which warms your hearts today. The teachers likewise feel, no doubt, the grateful sense of relief in the prospect of the vacation freedom and repose. Do these admissions compromise the old philosopher's conception of education as applied to our experience? Have we not these four years really been friends seeking happiness together?

There were, indeed, the first months of discovery and adjustment, months of a shy reserve which was as much a token of a delicate self-respect as of a natural timidity in a strange environment. The ruling impression was that all professors were middle-aged, learned and aloof, if not formidable. By and by the icy barriers began to melt down, first between student and student, and then between student and teacher. Common interests were discerned, the general ground of which came shortly to be illuminated by bright particular spots of personal attachment. Professors were found to possess, not only a bottle of the red ink of criticism, but also a can of the milk of human kindness, and, in their professional relations, to be concerned mainly to guide, to guard, and to serve—to be men, in short, frankly human-hearted, sensible, sympathetic, and accessible.

The happiness of the professor is that he works on the early, growing section of life's endless procession. He is always on the morning side of the planet. For him—

> Life's morning radiance hath not left the hills,
> Her dew is on the flowers.

Besides, "a college life is a life where it is easy and pleasant to practice benevolence and kindliness, and where a small investment of trouble pays a large percentage of happiness."

The fact of your happiness in the fellowships of student life is no less certain. Even now as you begin to sever the ties which four years of good comradeship have knitted, you feel it as never before, and as the separating years come and go with thronging cares and uncompanioned labor, it will grow in your memory yet more bright and precious.

But these personal relations in which we have found our happiness supply also the best part of our education. The drill in form and syntax and formula, the quiz and answer, the laboratory's precise observation and careful record, are good, but the touch of elbows which they involve is better; the touch of spirit is best. The less formal part of the education process is the more important. It is our fellowships that educate us. And this, not simply because, as Bacon says, "a man's wit and understanding doe clarifie and break up in communicating and discoursing with a friend, wherein he waxeth wiser than himself, and that more by an hour's discourse than by a day's meditation." It is rather because our fellowships make the opportunity for the subtle interplay of life upon life which is the heart of education. Our fellowships form our ideals, they infect us with their virtues or their vices, they set our standards, they determine our emotional attitudes, they fashion our life.

And the books which we read for culture—what are they but the extension of the range of personal fellowship? For a good book, as says Milton, is the precious life-blood of a master spirit, embalmed and treasured up on purpose to a life beyond life. Here again spirit touches spirit to enlarge and to vitalize, that is, to educate. One takes over as a personal experience Dante's lofty disdain of littleness, David's contrition, Carlyle's deep scorn of sham, Ruskin's openness to the beauty of the world, Browning's triumphant optimism.

> The drudging student trims his lamp,
> Opens his Plutarch, puts him in the place
> Of Roman, Grecian, draws the patched gown close,
> Dreams, "Thus should I fight, save or rule the world!"

If omniscience were the guide of life, if it were attainable, if it were even desirable, you might pride yourselves upon your precise acquisitions in letters and science. Permit me to remind you that these acquisitions are only the incidentals of education. The main question about you now is, not what you know, but how you feel. Not your information, but your attitude. Not your possessions, but your standards of value. Have you acquired here permanent intellectual interests and satisfactions? Do the things of the mind kindle your enthusiasm? Such a test and fine fruit of your student career is a testimony to the atmosphere of personal intercourse, the climate of opinion, in which you have lived. Do not be discouraged, therefore, if in the coming days you find your biology and geometry, your psychology and Latin and German drop piecemeal out of your mind; if you get to be unable to recall the names of half the books you have read; if you cannot quote Shakespeare and Tennyson with aptness and precision. You may forget your studies, but not the friends of your studies. You will not lose the outlook on life which you have acquired here, your inspirations, or your moral and spiritual alliances, and these be the great things, the determining things, in life.

Your Alma Mater hails you today with pride and congratulations. She crowns you today with the last token of her affection and confidence. She commends you today to your high task in the wider world.

12/26/38

CULTURE AND PRACTICAL EFFICIENCY

1909

By your grace and the authority of an inviolable tradition, I ask the privilege of the one word more.

In the lunette above the rostrum of the great hall in the College of the City of New York an American artist has painted a notable picture. Its title is "The Graduate." Behind the central glowing altar which illuminates all the scene sits "Wisdom" with a globe on her knees presenting the Western hemisphere. On either side of her pedestal extends a curved row of female figures which symbolize the great centers of learning, as Alexandria, Cordova, Bologna, Athens, Leyden, Heidelberg, and Oxford. In the foreground stands a capped and gowned incarnation of a radiant and victorious hope, with Alma Mater at his side bidding him forth to his career. Near at hand waits "Discipline" armed with sword and scourge to attend him wherever he may go. Students, aspirants, and representative immortals of all times are grouped about these central figures and watch the ceremonial with eager interest. Philosophy is there in the person of Democritus; law and the civic order, in Augustus Cæsar; science, in Galileo, Newton, Lavoisier, and Kelvin; the fine arts, in Beethoven and Michael Angelo; letters, in Petrarch and Shakespeare.

That great mural decoration is, of course, not in sight here today, but the scene and symbolism which it portrays are manifest palpably before us. The foreground of the picture is yours. You are starring in the center of the stage today as the protagonists of the action. Where you stand each with his torch just lit at the altar of Wisdom, a little pale perhaps and trembling at the gates of your career because you have not gone this way hitherto, the atmosphere is sweet with the sympathetic tenderness of gathered friends, and luminous with unseen but felt presences out of the realms of light come to receive you

[26]

into their fellowship and to hearten you for the long journey.

You do not need to be told that prophecy is already busy with your future, forecasting your diverging and various pathways. Possibly you have not discovered on the fringe of the encircling interest a calculating materialism shaking its head doubtfully, wishing you well indeed, but suspicious of your equipment—questioning whether your training these years in higher mathematics and alien tongues, in the remote theorizing of sociology, biology, and philosophy, constitutes a genuine preparation for the practical tasks which you are now to take up. Cap and gown, which now distinguish you, will later incommode you, and must be laid by. Is your scholarship a superficial, detachable garment, fine to shine in, but poor to work in? Have these four years sealed your compact with Discipline? And that torch of yours—did you really light it at the altar of Wisdom?

It may be worth while to consider the question thus presented, the question of the relation of a college career to a life career, of culture to practical efficiency. For the business world even yet very commonly agrees with the old banker in *The Mill on the Floss*, that young Tulliver's father went the wrong way to work in giving him an education for any manly business, looking after things and getting credit for what he did. When Tom had recited the list of his studies, including Euclid, Latin, Greek and Roman History, English poetry, Paley's Horæ Paulinæ, and Blair's Rhetoric, Uncle Deane, to whom he had applied for work, replied, "Well, you've had three years at these things—you must be pretty strong in 'em. Hadn't you better take up some line where they will come in handy?" Moreover, your own trepidation and embarrassment now as you pass to your work betray a sense of weakness, tinged at times with complaint of a traditional scheme of training which, you fear, trains for nothing.

Your own feeling is supported by current discussion, becoming daily more insistent, among men practically engaged in the work of education—discussion of the relatively slight connection which the college course makes with concrete opportunities in the life of the day. It urged that the Bachelor of Arts degree as we know it today was formed some hundreds of years ago when the materials of education were extremely meager. Since that time the most radical revolution within the limits of the human record has occurred, a marked feature of which was the multiplication of human interests and activities. And yet so authoritative has been the early model, and so conservative the college faculty, little change of that model to adjust it more vitally to the new complexion and content of our life has been allowed, except the chaos of the elective system. A former headmaster of Eton said not long ago: "One sees arrive here every year a lot of brisk, healthy boys with fair intelligence, and quite disposed to work, and at the other end one sees depart a corresponding set of young gentlemen who know nothing and can do nothing, and are profoundly cynical about all intellectual things." The same critical attitude is not without representation outside educational circles in the realm of letters. Here is your frank and deeply instructed essayist, Mr. Frederic Harrison, sneering at the culture of the schools as a desirable quality in a critic of new books, indeed, but, in practical public life, as simply a turn for small fault-finding, indecision, and love of selfish ease.

To this disparaging attitude, I am afraid, the noble tradition of culture in which your Alma Mater stands touching hands with Brown and Harvard and Oxford in a line of light all the way back to Alexandria and Athens, must make large concessions. You must agree, for example, that a genuine culture is attainable outside college precincts and by other than academic pathways. Witness numerous cases like Burns and Lincoln, who had little or no opportunity for formal education, and the late Carroll D. Wright, who, although he never went to college, received many college degrees and died as the President of Clark University. And not a few men having the

best of college opportunities, like Wordsworth and Browning
and Darwin,

> Did not love,
> Judging not ill perhaps, the timid course
> Of our scholastic studies,

and educated themselves outside and in spite of their pre-
scribed courses, or after they were ended.   By native aptitude
they have erected laboratories in woodsheds, by good luck they
have discovered the library.   An English sociologist has written sarcastically that there is a never-failing percentage of un-
dergraduates whom not even degrees and scholarships can keep
from the sources of culture.   On the other hand, many a man
after the most elaborate education finds himself grossly unedu-
cated.   Will you forgive me if I quote a remark of Sidney
Smith?   "Cambridge," said he, "is the wisest place in the
world, for the freshmen come up bearing stacks of wisdom,
and the seniors never carry any away."

Again, must not the warmest friend of culture make a further
concession, a psychological concession?   A narrow faith, says
Amiel, has more energy than an enlightened faith ; the world
belongs to will much more than to wisdom.   In delivering us
from error does not culture tend to paralyze life?   For example,
"Joan of Arc was not stuck at the cross-roads either by rejecting all the paths like Tolstoi, or by accepting them all like
Nietzsche.   She chose a path and went down it like a thunder-
bolt."   Too much knowledge is not good for the orator.   The
man of science may halt in doubt, or decline to form any opinion, because he knows so many possibilities of error.   A heightened and refined sensitiveness, a perception of the intricate
complexities of life, may lead to hesitation and inaction in the
conduct of life.   Know-all is the father of Do-nothing.

But when all reasonable concessions are made, and all possible derogations are allowed, when all is said, it remains in-
controvertible that college training does develop a sort of power
which is, as a rule, peculiar to itself.   It does create the pre-

sumption of positive achievement.   It is a genuine equipment.
The one per cent of American men who are liberally educated
hold forty per cent of the positions of trust and distinction.
Men of affairs are perceiving that the college-bred man, with
his knowledge of principles and his store of ideas, quickly commands the technique of an unfamiliar business, and, that once
mastered, outclasses his untrained competitor in practical efficiency.   Great economic enterprises are demanding more and
more a liberal culture as a foundation for special training, in
the case of the men they employ, and the college graduates
are responding by going directly into business in increasing
numbers.   For example, of the last Princeton class, fifty-six
entered business, twenty-two engineering, as against fifty-one
in law, and ten in the ministry.   A college man who fell to
drink has lately declared that two per cent of the "bowery
bums" who wait their turn in the New York bread line are
college men, but it was not their culture that brought them
down, but rather the absence of one of its elements.   For
strength of character is as truly a part of it as strength of intellect.

But to get and hold lucrative jobs cannot be counted the
best test of the efficiency of the genuinely cultivated man.
Any man's influence and activities lie in large measure outside his vocation.   His chief value and happiness originate,
not in his professional, but in his human relations of father,
brother, neighbor, citizen, teacher or guide.   It is precisely
in this section of life that culture finds its perfect work.   As it
is itself "the harmonious expansion of all the powers which
make the beauty and worth of human nature," culture touches
with blessing every human relation, inherits and carries forward the human tradition in the fullness of its riches, in civic
institutions, in art and letters, in science and religion.   This
sort of culture is as far as possible from the foolish pedantry
and the weak fastidiousness so often identified with it.   It embraces what biology would call health, what psychology would

call sanity, what ethics would call sympathy, and what religion would call holiness.   It is the sum of the elements of the higher life, and nothing else is to be compared with it for building up a complete human life, for beauty, for service, and for efficiency.

Your Alma Mater bids you forth to your career, charging you never to surrender your college idealism; charging you to preserve at all hazards the supremacy of life over living, of soul over sense.   You are more than your acquisitions, and your pressing problem will always be how with the soul it fares.   For—

> Still will the soul from its lone fastness high
>   Upon our life a ruling effluence send;
> And when it fails, fight as we will, we die,
>   And while it lasts, we can not wholly end.

CULTURE AND DEMOCRACY

1910

The daily paper of a leading American university reported last autumn that the father of one of the entering men presented at the registration office for execution the following legal instrument: "To whom it may concern: This is to certify that I have this day delivered to . . . University one boy, marked (name given), package unbroken and contents apparently sound and in good condition, value inestimable; said party of the second part to act *in loco parentis* for a period of six years, in consideration of divers sums paid by said party of the first part at stipulated intervals, and to return at expiration of that period one bachelor of laws, duly educated and certified, and otherwise uninjured."

Whether this statement is history or invention, it represents what really passes between father and college when the son first enters college. Four years ago such a contract was tacitly made in the case of each one of you. If this College, on its part, has fallen short of its obligation at any point, it is not because it has held its contract lightly or been indifferent to you. I propose now no examination in detail to verify the conviction which I must be content merely to announce, namely, that the "inestimable packages" received four years ago are today returned to expectant parents, not only certified bachelors of arts, science, and law, but, what is vastly more worth while, men of enhanced personal worth, of heightened efficiency for the life task wherever that task may lie. Fathers and mothers receive again their own with interest.

But you are also sons of a democracy. You came up hither out of that general equality of conditions which the eminent French critic of American institutions regarded as the fundamental fact of our social situation. Will you be at home in its bosom again? Do you return to it with unimpaired sympathy and allegiance? You have been greatly distinguished from the general body of your fellows and early associates. You have enjoyed privileges which scarcely one per cent of the country's population enjoy. Your studies have been in the liberal arts, which are quite beyond the reach of the average man. Your life here has been a special life, segregated to a degree and apart from the world. Have these distinctions built up a wall betwixt you and the world of men? Has your cultivation here narrowed or widened the range of your fellowship? Do you now pass out into an aristocracy of learning with no relations with the mass of men except as members of a class to govern them? How has your democracy fared at the hands of your culture?

If I might answer my own question, I should say that this four years' domination of your life and intellectual interests by the Wake Forest spirit leaves your sympathies quickened and wider ranging; your democracy has not suffered by the illumination of your culture. Culture would come too high, if it involved the compromise of democracy. For what is democracy? In etymology it is the rule of the people. But equal participation in government, manhood suffrage, and majority rule are not democracy itself so much as the mechanism of democracy. The essence of democracy is the spirit of fraternity and justice. It cannot be deceived by disguises of precedent and tradition, of circumstance and ceremony. It counts the individual human spirit so precious and so regal that its accidents of birth and position are insignificant. It was born into the modern world in the new definition of man in the teaching of Jesus, and its development through the Christian centuries is their shining distinction. The general struggle for freedom against despotism in all its forms has been universal and irresistible, possessing, as De Tocqueville says, all the characteristics of a divine decree. Next after religion, it is our dearest possession. We cannot afford to sacrifice it on the altar of culture.

And yet, not a few hold that the democratic ideal is in reality imperiled by college and university education. Higher education is sometimes flatly said to be aristocratic in tendency, and the perpetual elevation of entrance requirements and standards of graduation, together with the increasing cost of it, are cited in testimony. It is said, moreover, that the now fashionable endowment of higher education by plutocrats tends to confirm, if not to extend, the aristocracy of wealth by multiplying the number of dependents and sycophants. The General Education Board is a deep-laid scheme to establish the Rockefeller dynasty forever and ever. Its dupes are too eager for pelf to recognize the plot. It is urged, again, that the pomp and ceremony of academic occasions are an inheritance from the ecclesiastical hierarchy and a reflection of the arrogance and exclusiveness of kings' courts. In a sigh of surrender Dr. Slosson insists that a dozen mortar-boards on the campus are more of a menace to democracy than a million-dollar endowment from a trust magnate. Academic costume is an expression and advertisement of the academic spirit. There is yet another criticism lodged against higher education in its relation to democracy. The subjects of college study, more or less remote from the present-day occupations and interests of men, are held to foster a polite refinement of taste and manners which are more at home in the drawing-rooms of elegant leisure than in the cottages of the peasant and artisan, and if they fit for life at all, fit for the life of the limited professional class.

One could not hesitate to say that all these criticisms of college education are either baseless or extravagant. The raising of entrance requirements, for example, was the demand of the lower schools, and higher graduation standards have been the result of the assumption by the lower schools of work once classed as college work. The college course has been enlarged by so much, to the advantage of those who can take it at all, and their number has steadily increased.

The suggestion of the wholesale purchase of boards of trustees by Mephistophelian plutocrats to silence criticism, to control opinion, and to perpetuate the domination of ill-gotten wealth, is as absurd as it is odious. Those who make it do little credit either to their intelligence or to their independence.

Of academic costume it is, of course, to be remarked that it, like ordinary costume, is determined by fashion, and has no more significance for democracy than the costume requirements for special occasions outside the campus. The silk hats one sees in the processions on Pennsylvania Avenue at Presidential inaugurations—one could hardly think so many had been made the past decade by all the hat factories of the country. On such an occasion the silk hat is quite democratic. Dr. Slosson reminds one of Touchstone in the extravagant significance which he attaches to the prescriptions of college etiquette by no means universal. "Why," argues Touchstone to the simple shepherd, "if thou never wast at court, thou nevei sawest good manners; if thou never sawest good manners, then thy manners must be wicked; and wickedness is sin, and sin is damnation. Thou art in a parlous state, shepherd."

As to the college course of study, it has to be said that, even in the former time of its rigidity and aloofness, it had representatives in all careers, and, with the exception of teaching, it had little more relation to the learned professions than to the unlearned. The body of knowledge which it bestowed was in great part promptly dropped in all. Only its training and general culture remained as a permanent possession. But in the past forty years the ideal of the cultivated man has undergone a genuine reconstruction. His interests are now conceived to be coextensive with the reach of intelligence. He is no fastidious pedant. He assumes no critical airs or cynical superiority. His mark is not scholarship so much as power for service. He exhibits not so much a specific equipment as a wide-eyed, general alertness and adaptive capacity. To quote Charles W. Eliot, he is "a man of quick perceptions, broad sympathies, and wide affinities; responsive, but independent; self-reliant, but deferential; loving truth and candor, but also moderation and proportion; courageous, but gentle; not finished, but perfecting. All authorities agree that true culture is not exclusive, sectarian, or partisan, but the very opposite; that it is not to be attained in solitude, but in society; and that the best atmosphere for culture is that of a school, university, academy, or church, where many pursue together the ideals of truth, righteousness, and love."

Such an ideal of culture, it must be apparent, is in thorough harmony with the democratic ideal. And whatever may have been true of the narrow scope and rigid curriculum of the old-time college, there can be little doubt that the modern college is the most democratic of social institutions. This is especially true of the small college like ours, where conditions are simple and where intimate acquaintance throughout the student body makes recognition on other grounds than those of merit and personal worth impossible.

It ought to be added that the aim of culture and the aim of democracy are at bottom the same. It has been said that democracy cannot be disentangled from an aspiration toward human perfectibility. Certainly culture is animated by the same hope; it is a progressive movement in the same direction. The principle of democracy, said Montesquieu, is virtue. It is equally true that the finest fruit of culture is character.

And so today your Alma Mater after four years of nourishing and guidance, years of constantly deepening interest in you, gives you back to the democracy out of which you are sprung confirmed in your allegiance to its spirit and aims, and equipped to serve its ends of fraternity and justice. She enjoins upon you that you take up the social and civic responsibility which your training imposes, that you bear a part, a worthy part, in the social amelioration which is the concern and the glory of our time; that you seek to make your home, your neighborhood, your town, your State, your country, "a prosperous province of the Kingdom of God." She invokes upon every one of you the fullness of the divine benediction; she pledges you in this parting moment her unbroken interest and affection, and ventures to hope that she may prove increasingly worthy of your loyalty and devotion.

CULTURE AND RELIGION

1911

In Brittany, that picturesque and remote corner of France, where the sea bites hungrily into the land, where fairy wands are still potent and legend has the semblance and authority of history, the fishermen tell the story of a city called Is, which was long ago swallowed up by the sea. They say that its church spires can be seen in the hollows of the waves when the sea is rough, and in calm weather the music of its church bells can be heard above the waters. The eminent skeptical critic, Renan, was reared in this region, and in its narrow and simple atmosphere took the first steps of his preparation for the career of a Catholic priest. He himself tells us that at fifteen and a half years of age, without warning, he was thrust from the most obscure of little towns in the most obscure of provinces into the vortex of all that was most sprightly and alert in Parisian society, with sights and experiences as novel to him as if he had suddenly landed in France from Tahiti or Timbuctoo. This abrupt transplanting of the young Breton priest was the crisis of his career. The new life, elaborate and splendid, the new religion, bedecked with ribbons and scented with musk, the expanding horizon of the new knowledge, were at once fascinating and intolerable. For with the idealism and tenderness of his mystic race, he loved his mother and his mother's simple and unperplexed religion, and this great Paris in a way compromised both. The passing years deepened the contrast between the Christianity of Brittany and the Christianity of the capital. Both systems of belief fell more and more into discredit before his growing critical faculty, and were ultimately abandoned. He at length counted himself no longer a Christian. And yet the imperious and fundamental hunger of the heart asserts itself now and again, and that early sense of God and the eternal things which is, I apprehend, the

[38]

essence of faith. In the "Recollections of My Youth," he says, "I feel that my existence is governed by a faith which I no longer possess," and recalling the legend of the submerged city of the Breton fishermen, "I often fancy that I have at the bottom of my heart a city of Is, with its bells calling to prayer a recalcitrant congregation."

The brilliant and unhappy Frenchman has not been alone in finding a new environment the judge and despoiler of the old. Most men, in fact, find such transitions difficult and dangerous in proportion to their violence. The difficulty lies in making the adjustment to the new situation, the danger in the possibility of losing in the process of adjustment some of the treasures of the past. I do not doubt that you who pause here today on the verge of such an experience as you pass out of college to your life career, had four years ago when you entered the college the same sort of experience—had your freshman difficulties of adjustment, sophomoric, professorial, and other difficulties. But I am not thinking now of your adaptation troubles in particular, but rather of the other aspect of the transition. I beg to bring to your attention the peril of the widened horizon which you have faced in your college course. We doubtless agree upon the important advantage of the larger outlook on man and nature. I am asking, what have you surrendered to secure it? It has come dear to some men. They have bartered for it their native love of beast and bird, the forest, the soil and all the fair things which spring out of it, their wholesome joy in the simple associations of their youth, now grown empty and commonplace. Some have contracted the bookworm disease, one of whose chief symptoms is the loss of the noble capacity of enthusiasm and all vital interest in the practical concerns of life. Some, in the enlightenment of the wider vision, have lost the energy of their narrower faith, and some have suffered the last great disaster— they have lost their faith itself. How, my brothers, has it been with you? How long is the inventory of your losses? What

are the items? The time for self-gratulation upon winning
diplomas in this college is hardly come until you have made
up this inventory.

You will allow me, in these last words, to be direct and personal. I am chiefly concerned to raise the question of the
effect of your culture upon your religion.

> You've seen the world—
> The beauty and the wonder and the power,
> The shapes of things, their colors, lights and shades,
> Changes, surprises.

Are you able to add, with Browning's worldly-minded Lippo,
"And God made it all"? Or are you finding it hard to hold
on to your pre-collegiate religious beliefs?

There are two explanations of the religious crisis of the college student. The college period is the time of the widened
horizon. Well-nigh the whole series of the early intellectual
conceptions get then either their expansion or their correction.
Not a few of them are seen to be incompatible with what one
learns in college, and, being woven into the tissue of religious
beliefs, they involve the whole tissue in their own discredit.
If geology forces the extensions of the earth's history beyond
six thousand years, a new interpretation of Genesis or the surrender of its inspiration appears to be necessitated, and in either
case an earlier religious conception goes. If biology presents
evolution as the method of the creation, the first result of the
new idea is the question whether there is then any Creator.
That sort of thing is not many times repeated before a general
skeptical attitude toward the whole body of religious beliefs
comes to be established. A second related college experience
tends to produce the same attitude, namely, the exclusive preoccupation with intellectual interests and the consequent enrichment of the intellectual life, while the neglected spiritual
nature remains at the old level. The discrepancy is unfavor-
able to religion and the old ideas associated with it.

Let me remind you that, in this matter as in all others, the college is not apart from the world, but is a section of it, and that such an individual experience as I have sketched is an epitome of the racial experience at the successive levels of its advancing culture. The single illustration of the scientific revolution may be cited. The elaboration of opinion under religious sanction had ranged over well-nigh the whole world of fact. It involved cosmogony, ethnology, and history. It had its theory of the earth and of the heavens, of disease, of language, of education. But these matters were manifestly within the scope of science and subject to its revision. Accordingly, when the new science of the last century met this crystalized body of pre-scientific opinion which had developed under the sanction of Christianity, a conflict was inevitable. The eventual issue of the conflict might have been foreseen. The set of opinions more or less closely associated with the Christian life was revised and given a fresh statement more nearly in accord with the fresh knowledge of the time, and we learned anew to make the important distinction between the religious experience and a theory of the religious experience, between religion and theological speculation about religion.

I speak of this adjustment as accomplished, and so it is. And yet even now one hears occasionally from certain quarters of the horizon echoes of that conflict as still unsettled. Similarly, as individuals, we appear to be unable to learn by the experience of others, but must needs each one for himself repeat the experience. Every generation of college students gets its case of doubts at least by the junior year, and just as regularly passes through the storm and stress period into a large place where faith is as intelligent as it is firm. I hope that you, without exception, have completed safely the transition from your Brittany to your Paris and find now your religion at home with your culture. For culture without religion is partial, unsatisfying, unsafe. Religion without culture is partial, austere, superstitious. Combine them, not in a weak amalgam, but each at the top of its development, and you lead the happy and victorious life.

Press out and out the limits of your culture. Establish, if you can, outposts in every province of intellectual achievement. Do not be afraid to look into any dark corner or to walk on any of the far-looking heights of God's world, and you will find Him everywhere in proportion to the keenness of your penetration and the breadth of your outlook. And finding Him, keep to the shelter and inspiration of His companionship all the long way you go. So will you discover the burden which He imposes to be your strength, and the struggle your triumph.

CULTURE AND SERVICE

1912

The seal impressed on the diplomas which you have just received bears the early Christian symbol, the monogram of the Greek form of Christ with the Greek Alpha and Omega. The rays of light issuing from the monogram recall that Christ is the light of the world, and the whole suggests that Wake Forest College is one of the agents of its dissemination *"Pro Humanitate"*—for the benefit of mankind. The seal is not an artist's empty fancy. It was designed to present the facts of history. This symbolism and motto set forth the conscious aim and function of the College.

A correspondent of a northern journal the year when the institution was opened, after a depressing view of conditions in North Carolina, adds, "They have kindled a light in the Wake Forest Institute which will, I trust, soon shed its beams over the whole State." That is precisely it; light for service. And the men who kindled that flickering torch seventy-eight years ago were moved by the Christian impulse. Wake Forest was not alone in this regard. Harvard College (1636) was born in the pious wish "to vindicate the truth of Christ and promote His glorious Kingdom." Yale College (1701) was founded, as says the original charter, in "a sincere regard to and zeal for the upholding and propagating of the Christian Protestant religion." With the single exception of the University of Pennsylvania (1751), all collegiate institutions up to the middle of the nineteenth century were almost wholly Christian in origin. Even now, in spite of secular influence invading after that date the older foundations and dominating many of the later ones, three fourths of the existing higher institutions of learning have sprung from denominational effort. In other words, Christ is still King in American college education, and

the promotion of His Kingdom is the avowed prime business
of the American college.

Do such an origin and relation fetter the spirit of American
youth? or compromise freedom of inquiry? or put the bushel
over the light of truth? Let the most influential thinker in
the World's Congress of Free Christianity and Religious Progress, meeting in Berlin two years ago, make answer. "We can
be sure," says Troeltsch, "that European culture without a
foundation in the religious power of Christianity can scarcely
endure." Let western civilization itself make answer, for all
which distinguishes and glorifies it is directly due to that stream
of altruism with which Christianity has enriched every stage
of its development. Consider, moreover, the fundamental and
comprehensive character of the Kingdom of God. It is the
organic expression of the will of God in human relations, in
all human relations. Its demand reaches to the roots of being.
Its supreme sanction is the vital bond of all social organization.
The authority of its law is universal, controlling all life, individual and national, and its race-wide sway is the inspiration
and goal of all the highest human endeavor. It involves love
of family, love of country, love of humanity. It contemplates
a personal and social regeneration, and lays a firm hand on
things as they are to make them what they ought to be. Its
standard in the midst of a society still largely pagan has created
the social problem, and from the practical ministry to all human
need which that standard enjoins there is no release.

If, now, Wake Forest College sprang out of the bosom of
this large conception, if it is called into the service of this divine purpose, what is the instrument of its service? by what
means does it seek to realize its aim? It may be answered
shortly, by culture. Not so much by discovering new truth
as by imparting the Christian ideal, for its interest is not in
subjects, but in men. It *cultivates* not literature and science,
but men. And cultivation always counts.

The grapes which dye thy wine are richer far,
Through culture, than the wild wealth of the rock ;
The suave plum than the savage-tasted drupe ;
The pastured honey-bee drops choicer sweets,
The flowers turn double, and the leaves turn flowers.

What we call *culture* the ancient Latins called *humanitas*, a word which brings to the front an essential quality of culture, namely, freedom from prejudice and provincialism, a wide expansiveness of sympathies. The pursuit of the branches of polite learning has, indeed, sometimes issued in a fastidious superiority which held aloof from the mass of humanity, if, indeed, it did not despise its rude manners, its commonplace thoughts, and its empty interests. But such a dainty product of mere literary and æsthetic pursuits is not culture. It lacks the root idea of *humanitas*. Beside this humanness and catholicity of feeling, culture recognizes the supremacy of the soul as against the insistence of sense, and imposes a lofty, unselfish life ideal. It enhances the excellence of our nature in its harmonious expansion. If we may follow Mr. Matthew Arnold, it involves the scientific passion of pure knowledge, the moral and social passion for doing good, for removing human error, clearing human confusion, and diminishing human misery, the desire to make reason and the will of God prevail. Such culture, he adds, is of the highest practical service. It is equally apparent that such culture is the proper instrument by which the College may realize its high mission as an agent of the Kingdom for the benefit of mankind.

The opportunity for this service has never been larger or more inspiring than it is today. Here is the needy state calling for equipped men of patriotism and character to serve the people in legislation and administration. One of the most pleasing things in more recent Wake Forest history is the increasing number of our men who are carrying the Wake Forest ideal into the service of the State. But the public life of the college man is by no means restricted to official position. In-

deed, the modern democratic state is not governed by its officers, but by its atmosphere, by the subtle, pervasive, universal
power of public opinion. And the responsibility to guide and
to correct this king of the new democracy falls heavily upon
you and those who share with you the privilege of college education. There is pressing demand for the building up of a
public conscience on the civic obligations of wealth, on sanitation and the battle to eradicate infectious diseases, on the insane perpetuation of degeneracy through unrestricted independence in the matter of marriage eligibility. The enemies
of the life of man, some of them entrenched in vested interests
or deep-set in an inveterate aristocratic tradition—who will
meet them in the open field of mortal combat but the men who
have the college equipment and the college ideal? And the
enemies of the social order—that monstrous irrationality, war,
which carries commercialism to the extreme of social suicide—
what can break its back but the idealism and intelligence of
the college men of the world, who are now finding in the new
patriotism a new arena for the martial virtues? Social injustice wherever it may appear; the arrogance and oppression
of corporate wealth; the hard conditions under which the poor
fight the endless battle for bread; the cry of little children
for their inalienable rights of playtime and education: here,
gentlemen, is no small part of your task and your opportunity
to push forward the growing Kingdom of God, the reign of
righteousness and peace.

And permit me to remind you that a high purpose and a
true ideal, a good equipment and a recognized task, amount
to little unless thay are hooked up and take hold on the actual
situation at the place of most urgent need. Those famous
North Carolina resolutions which, more than a year before
the national declaration of independence, declared the commissions of the king and parliament annulled, appointed in
resolution number twenty Colonel Thomas Polk and Dr.
Joseph Kennedy to purchase 300 pounds of powder, 600 pounds

of lead, and 1,000 flints! Lay aside cap and gown, get your
gun and fill your powder horn. The enemy is trampling
down the corn, looting the precious personal wealth of your
State and country. Out with you for game, in the name of
God and humanity! The fight will call for all your heroism
and enthusiasm. It will be protracted, often acute and dangerous. I would hearten you for it by reminding you that you
will find your life in proportion as you lose it, and that you
fight no hopeless battle; the bugles of God never sound retreat.
The universe is keyed to righteousness, and as certainly as God
is in His heaven, all will be right with the world.

In 1848, with French troops beleaguering the city of Rome,
Mazzini rebuked the quarreling and irresolute deputies, saying, "Here in Rome we may not be moral mediocrities."
It is even so: to have been noble once imposes a perpetual
obligation of nobleness. It belongs to the blood, and ever to
be base is a form of suicide. So is a commonwealth under
bonds to its heroic past. With Quaker and Baptist independence in the East truckling to no foreign-bred aristocracy, civil
or religious; with King's Mountain and the Mecklenburg
Resolves in the west, and Guilford Courthouse in the center;
with her gray jackets in the sixties outnumbering her ballots,
and her Lane and Pettigrew on the fiery crest of Gettysburg,
North Carolina is irrevocably committed to the highest civic
virtues, and her sons to the unbroken tradition of heroism.

According to her opportunity, if not according to her hope,
your Alma Mater has led you into this heritage of inspiration;
has imparted to you freely of her ideal of *humanitas pro humanitate;* has enriched you with inward resources and satisfactions
against transient depression or defeat; has equipped you with
the implements of victory, and now sends you forth her latest
and her largest addition to the forces of the new patriotism.
"And whosoever would be first among you shall be servant
of all."

CULTURE AND PUBLIC LIFE

1913

"I long not only to burgeon, but also to bear fruit to the public advantage."—*Dante, De Monarchia, I, 1.*

There are a thousand definitions of education. It is said to be, for example, the process of filling up, of drawing out, of equipping to make a living, of equipping for life. This last definition is not far from Ruskin's view: "You do not educate a man by telling him what he knew not, but by making him what he was not." Education "makes" a man in the sense of bringing him into intelligent and sympathetic relation with the total life of the race of which he is a member. Such a relation of adjustment is an essential condition of life. The interests and achievements of the race are numerous and varied, but they may be all reduced to these five groups: Religion, which controls all with a sovereign pervasive power, Letters, Science, Art, and Social Institutions.

Life itself is adjustment to its environment. Fullness of life is in proportion to range of adjustment. But this conception is too negative to satisfy the ideal of the highest life. It is not enough to enter profitably into the racial inheritance, and to transmit it unimpaired to those who follow. It ought to be enriched and extended. You agree, but protest that only the genius could be expected to do so. "You do not expect me to give a new interpretation of religion, prove a second St. Francis, who is said to have listened to those to whom God Himself would not listen. I cannot aspire to lighten the burdens on the back of labor, to enlarge the boundaries of human knowledge, to invent a new poetic form or a new style of architecture, or to set a new standard for the art of Praxiteles or Titian!" But you may, in your own person, illustrate the standards which are now the glory of our humanity, and so increase the number of examples which constitute the wealth

of our inheritance.   Moreover, taking your place in the social
order with the light of history at command, with intellectual
equipment for the largest social service, and the Christian ideal
and impulse to inspire and direct it, you may react positively
upon your environment.   You are not only able to correct
social wrong and improve life conditions, but you are under
the highest obligations so to do.   To whom much is given, of
him shall much be required.

But I beg to turn your thought upon a special obligation
which your culture imposes—the obligation of service in public
life.

It is said to be bad form in the Scandinavian states to be
known as an office-seeker.   Somewhat of the same discredit
attaches to the "professional politician," that is, to the man
who, with little regard to the question of fitness for public
duty, adopts the political career for purely private ends.   And
in not a few cases the men who are worthiest of public trust
have been effectually deterred by the reputation and methods
of unscrupulous politicians.   This aloofness from public life
on the part of men called into it by character and training has
made the opportunity for political pillage which never goes
begging.   And so our finest men are not infrequently in a sort
of alliance with our worst men for the perpetuation of social
waste and injustice, and must accept a part of the responsibility
for the official meanness and self-seeking of which they com-
plain.

But the situation is rapidly changing.   We are not likely to
go the full length with Aristotle, who held politics to be the
highest intellectual discipline inasmuch as it was concerned
with the good of the community, which was the supreme practical end of life.   Ethics and education, which both took orders
from politics, he treated as branches of this noble discipline.
In his view the individual life had neither goodness nor significance apart from the State.   But we shall have to agree
with this "master of those who know" when he defines man

4

as a political animal capable of full development only in the
association of community life. Certainly it is this community
life which is coming to rule our thinking. Individualism has
had its day, a noble and most important day. It established
for good and all the independence and moral competency of
the social unit, and now, with that superlative achievement
to its credit, it is giving place to collectivism. "Every man
must bear his own burden"—that is individualism. "Bear ye
one another's burdens"—that is collectivism. The contacts of
life were never so numerous as now. Communication was
never so rapid or so universal. The freedom with which the
products of labor are exchanged is extending the principle of
the division of labor into an unprecedented minuteness of spe-
cialism and forcing men into coöperation and interdependence.
No man liveth to himself. With a new emphasis it may be
said today that one man is no man. The sense of brotherhood
and mutual dependence is growing apace. We are discovering the necessity and advantage of coöperation in agriculture
and industry, in education and religion. Men are moving as
never before in masses. Social questions are to the fore, and
individual conduct is coming to be judged after Aristotle's
method.

In this general atmosphere public position is acquiring a
new dignity. It means more than ever it meant. Its opportunity of genuine service is larger, and the public conscience
respecting it is more alert and exacting. Illustrations abound.
Witness the widespread movement to put the administration
of municipal affairs on a business footing; the organization of
training schools for public service; municipal efficiency commissions and bureaus of municipal research; the short ballot
reform, which proposes to make minor officers responsible to
the major officers who appoint them, and so diminish the
patronage and influence of convention and primary bosses.
Witness the relentless investigation of insurance and other
corporation methods, of election scandals and land frauds, and

recall the popular revulsion and resentment at the disclosures which followed. And our general political history tells the same story. The reconquest by the people of their political rights and powers within the past dozen years has been called our second war of independence, so rapid and revolutionary has it been. It is not the result of party agitation, but rather of the new public conscience which is calling both parties to repentance. There is everywhere a new sense of public responsibility, a new impatience of venality and trimming, a new affirmation of democracy. A boundless scorn of favoritism is driving old leaders off the stage, and "honest, patriotic, and forward-looking men" are taking their places.

What a brilliant senator said some years ago about the irrelevancy of the Ten Commandments in the sphere of politics could not be said today, for the moral character of all public problems is now a commonplace of political thinking. Social injustice is the fruit of moral evil, and no question which concerns the well-being of men, women, and children can be settled at all until it is settled in righteousness. Child labor, war, and protected vice only need to face the commandment "Thou shalt not kill." The ancient law "Thou shalt not steal" reduces the tariff from the category of problem to the category of crime. The troubles of capital and labor will be composed when justice reigns in both realms.

Now the government is the apparatus adopted by the people for the settlement of these questions in the interest of the people. It is the enlightenment of the people, their moral and social standards, that make the government, and the government is no better and no worse than the people. Its only function is the social good. It exists for the people, not the people for it. It is directly concerned with social improvement, and when its administration is inefficient or perverted, social disasters result which require generations to repair. Politics may be defined as the principles of civil government and the conduct of state affairs, the making and administration of public policies.

My practical question to you is, who should make and administer these policies? The cultured or the illiterate? The provincial-minded or the far-seeing and open-minded? The coarse-fibred spoilsmen, who consider public office not a public trust but a financial opportunity, or the men of moral enthusiasm and the divine trait of self-surrender for the good of others? To state these alternatives is to choose between them. And you see their drift. Is it not straight to you? You cannot escape the "responsibility of excellence." Under this constraint many of you, after some ripening of experience, must put your "boy heart," to quote the phrase of last evening's superb address, your "open mind," your "disciplined thought," your "larger vision," and your "higher ideal" at the service of the State, and swell the already large number of Wake Forest men who adorn the public life of the Commonwealth and the Nation. And the rest of you in other posts of service, with your several endowments, will fight the enemies of human life by whatever names they may be called, give yourselves wholeheartedly to all noble philanthropies and all forms of social betterment, and contribute your decisive part to the formation of that public opinion which is the king of democracy.

In commenting upon the literary form of a notable address of Lord Morley's, an English paper was tempted to lament the loss which the world of letters sustained when that great man took to politics, but it reflected that the suggestion was an unworthy one, for, said the editor, what could a man do better with his genius than devote it to the service of his country?

> Thyself and thy belongings
> Are not thine own so proper as to waste
> Thyself upon thy virtues, they on thee.
> Heaven doth with us as we with torches do,
> Not light them for themselves; for if our virtues
> Did not go forth of us, 'twere all alike
> As if we had them not. Spirits are not finely touched
> But to fine issues.

CULTURE AND FREEDOM

1914

The ancestry of the Bachelor of Arts degree may be traced back through the dominance of the Greek and Roman literature of the Renaissance, the seven so-called liberal arts of Cassiodorus of the sixth century, the nine liberal arts of the old Roman, Varro, to the "liberal" education of Aristotle and Plato. The specific content of this education varied from period to period, but its controlling conception throughout its long history is directly descended from the antithesis which these Greek philosophers set up between the life of elegant leisure and contemplation appropriate to a free man and the sordid and menial life of the slave. Certain "useful" subjects, as reading and writing, bodily culture, music, and drawing, they admitted to the curriculum because of their higher value for the formation of taste, character, and intellectual refinement; but mechanical crafts and what we call professional studies, whose value was merely commercial, they held to be illiberal, as the practice of them set a stamp on the body and restricted the outlook of the mind. "Liberal" education, on the other hand, as the name suggests, was such as tended to make its recipient a free man in body and soul and fit him for the full citizenship of a state. The "liberal arts" cultivated by the freeman and philosopher were divorced from the practical activities of the world, and so it came to pass that the Bachelor of Arts of the later time passed out of college into life to discover that he had been occupied with intellectual pursuits more or less remote from the interests to which he must henceforth devote himself.

The standard requirements of the Bachelor of Arts degree were established before the scientific revolution of the last century. That revolution was without precedent in its enormous multiplication of human interests and activities, and it distinctly widened, of course, the hiatus between college and life. The Bachelor of Arts tradition, consolidated by centuries of refined conservatism, held on its way with remarkable persistence, submitting but slowly to the forcible trespass of the new subjects, which came, under the Harvard leadership, to be known as electives. But the widest range of electives has failed to close the hiatus and now bears the additional discredit of relaxing the severe and wholesome discipline of the old standards and dissipating in numerous superficialities the solid attainment for which the old degree was the universal symbol.

This is the fourth session since the Wake Forest faculty introduced a new scheme of studies organized in the hope of solving, at least in part, this pressing problem. Subjects of universal human interest, as opposed to special vocational interest, were required of all students. They occupy the first two years of the course and are supposed to recognize with due respect the honorable Bachelor of Arts tradition. Among the other subjects, legitimate and numerous as they were, choice was allowed, but the choice was controlled and directed into channels which pass without interruption into the student's life career. These subjects, occupying the last two years of the course, were assembled into seven groups, each of which, without loss of culture value, is characterized by its relation to some leading vocation. It is among these groups that the student makes his choice, not indiscriminately among many unrelated subjects.

The Class of 1914 is the first whose studies have been wholly ordered under this scheme. Permit me to raise the question whether the new curriculum, judged by its product, is entitled to be called "liberal." Has the truth so known, while serving to connect your training with your task, done for you the supreme service of making you free? For of what avail is any amplitude of training, if your task is a servitude? What matters dexterity of hand or nimbleness of mind, if either wears a chain?

Of those great gifts of life—Knowledge, Beauty, Freedom—the greatest is Freedom. Knowledge may be wide as Nature and deep as the soul of man, but if it be not free, free to speak, free to serve, what doth it profit? And Beauty which is not free to run out into line and tint and tone is a vain abstraction. Even life itself, whose first demand is that it be full—filled out to its proper sphere on every radius of capacity, life will fail of fulfillment unless it be free. And culture, which is the enhancement of life, the moulding of life to all excellencies, is no culture, if it be not liberal, that is to say, emancipating.

Blackstone will tell you that natural liberty consists in acting as one thinks fit without any restraint or control except by the law of nature, but that every man, when he enters society, gives up a part of his liberty. Civil liberty, accordingly, is natural liberty so far restrained by human laws, and no farther, as is expedient for the public advantage. Where there is no law, he continues, there is no freedom. A famous annotator adds, "The liberty of doing everything which a man's passions urge him to attempt, or his strength enables him to effect, is savage ferocity; it is the liberty of a tiger, and not the liberty of a man." For the present purpose we may agree that freedom is self-determination in harmony with the laws of life, the inner mind consenting to the outer ordinance. And so a free man is one who, in a real sense, is master of his own thought and action, but who, nevertheless, is under the restraint of his social and divine relations; and he will be the last to challenge the dictum of Burke, that liberty must be limited in order to be possessed.

According to this standard, do you adjudge yourselves to be free men today? I do not ask whether you count graduation day as emancipation day. I am concerned, rather, with the results of your four years' campaign here in quest of freedom. As you canvass the records today, do you find the memorials of an enlarging self-mastery, of a progressive emancipation? Have the Wake Forest curriculum, atmosphere, and fellowships proved efficient in breaking the chains of any slavery with which you came here, in dissolving any alien usurpations in your life?

An emancipating culture will advertise and justify itself in all the sections of our nature. Body culture should issue in physiological freedom; mind culture, in intellectual freedom; conscience culture, in moral freedom; soul culture, in spiritual freedom.

Physiological freedom. The educated man of the twentieth century is not anaemic, languishing in a washed-out, wan vitality. He is a better animal at graduation than at matriculation. His physical culture has corrected the defects of development, made weakness strong, deepened the red of the blood, accumulated a surplus of nervous energy, and sends him out of college with a health and vigor which are the token of the law of liberty written in his members—the liberty to function without perversion or excess. He has realized the truth of Rousseau's paradox, "the weaker the body the more it commands; the stronger the body, the better it obeys," and with Rabbi Ben Ezra he cries:

> All good things
> Are ours, nor soul helps flesh more, now, than flesh helps soul.

Intellectual freedom. The greatest of the old Greeks said that the slave is one who in his actions does not express his own ideas, but those of some other man. In so far as you are phonographs speaking out of you only what is spoken into you, if you are not voices, but echoes, if your beliefs in any realm whatsoever are still traditional and not personal, if you are still capable of subscribing discreetly to propositions which you have not taken the trouble to understand, your culture is so far defective, and an inscribed bit of skin cannot hide the marks of your slavery. If you are your own master, you will have your own view.

Moral freedom. There can be no virtue except in the atmosphere of freedom. Morality has been defined as free obedience to a self-imposed law. We are bound indissolubly to our past, but we are not bound hopelessly by it. The dreadfull facts of our entanglement in matter are elements in the epic of our self-deliverance, but our deliverance is not fully achieved until we are free, not only from the shackles of our lower nature, but also from the prescriptions of an external legislation, and we do right not according to precedent or command, but as the free expression of an inward preference.

Spiritual freedom is the sum and pledge of all other freedoms. A culture which leaves the soul in bondage is partial and insecure. It cannot so much as guarantee its triumphs in the lower ranges of our nature. And strange as it may appear, in this region the yoke is the symbol of our liberation. The denial of self becomes the largest affirmation of self. It is the higher self which denies the lower. Against the usurping self the real self publishes its declaration of independence. You lose your life to find it; lose it to an overmastering ideal, and recover it transfigured by that ideal; lose it to a heroic cause, and recover it invested with the heroism which it sought to promote; lose it to a great and noble friendship, and recover it your very own, but participating in the greatness and nobleness of your infinite Friend. Make yours the prayer of the Indian poet-philosopher, "Let only that little of my fetters be left whereby I am bound with thy will, and thy purpose is carried out in my life—and that is the fetter of thy love." For if the Son shall make you free, you shall be free indeed.

CULTURE AND LEADERSHIP

1915

A tradition which I can neither break nor evade requires of me a parting word. It can only gather up in convenient form for review and summary the ideals and aims which this College has sought to grow in you these four years past.

The College was founded against the pressure of hard external conditions. The casting vote of William D. Moseley, of the North Carolina Senate, was needed to legitimate its birth. Its immediate friends were few and scattered and not overburdened with excess of fortune. But the inward pressure of a great ideal prevailed, and provision not meagre for its day was made for education under Christian auspices and for Christian aims. You stand in this honorable succession and pass out today to recruit the forces enlisted for the renewal of the social order after the Christian standard.

The good Providence which picked you out of the mass of your fellows in the ratio of one out of a hundred to profit by such opportunities as you have had here was not concerned primarily for you, but for the better service which you might render the higher aims of life. You may have come here at first to enhance your power of acquisition and to enlarge your capacity of enjoyment, but, I charge you, if you leave these halls now with such a selfish view of your college training, you demonstrate at once your unworthiness and our defeat. College training does, indeed, enlarge the capacity of enjoyment, it does enhance the power of acquisition, but college training under Christian guidance and control submits the enriched personality to the Christian aim and holds itself open to the Christian demand for service at the point of need.

Culture is the call to leadership; Christian culture to the leadership of the forces of righteousness. Our most respected publicist has said that the future of democracy is with the schools. But I venture to think that light is not the only need of democracy. Light is good, but air is essential. Religion is the breath of democracy. Culture apart from the Christian motive merely equips with a higher efficiency a selfish individualism, which written large spells anarchy. But as religion is the bond of all social aggregates, so culture which is under the sway of the Christian ideal is the instrument to transform democracy into Christian democracy and establish it in perpetuity.

Such a culture is marked by a store of ideas gathered out of all the fields of human interest and activity, and so it is not nonplussed in a new situation, is capable of prompt adjustment, is fertile of suggestion, with the result of passing in any group not so trained into a natural leadership. It is an inner discriminating taste, openness of mind which looks abroad with sympathetic appreciation and appropriates what is serviceable to its ends from any quarter whatsoever. The disguise of different names cannot hide it from essential unity of purpose, or discharge it from a friendly coöperation. It hates error, but would not burn people; it hates error, but knows enough to recognize its own fallibility. Without self-assertion it rides abroad redressing human wrong, and like Sir Galahad its strength is as the strength of ten because its heart is pure. What the old Spanish knight said in empty bombast, Christian culture says with a chastened sense of responsibility, "I was born into an age of iron to transform it into an age of gold."

Permit me to specify the spheres where culture consecrated to the noblest ends will exercise its natural leadership.

The enemies of human life are numerous and persistent, and they take their toll with a certainty and regularity capable of being set down in statistical tables beforehand. Their challenging gauntlet lies on the threshold of your career. Some of them attack the standard and type of the race; some of them menace or mar the social order. For example, we have learned but lately that half our illness and a third of our deaths are preventable ; that we do not live out our proper expectancy ; that many a prolonged life limps at its task on a low level of efficiency, and that few even of the most vigorous ever reach the normal level. We have learned, moreover, that the human being capitalized merely as working power has five times the value of all other capital. Take up that gauntlet : fight the indifference of the government which, to protect us from enemies mainly imaginary, spends seventy per cent of its revenue, but to protect human life from disease and forestall defects which put ten per cent of the population on the backs of the rest, spends one and a third per cent of its revenue. Fight the indifference of the local public and the popular superstition that mortality statistics reflect the divine decree.

An even more serious enemy of the standard of the race is vice. It is the function of the young, as a thoughtful writer has observed, to equip each generation with gaiety, to assert the worth of life, against the disillusionment of age. But an industrial period is more interested in the productive labor of the young, who flock to industrial centers under hazardous conditions. The elemental love of play and the elemental sex susceptibility are commercialized on the horrible assumption that there can be no joy which is not impure, no gaiety which is not a debauch. Pick up that gauntlet and let gallantry reinforce intelligence as you ferret out and strike down this darkest foe of the race.

Alcoholism is a vulgarity, but it is more. It is an enemy of the race. You will be expected to help make the spreading victory against it complete. Gambling is a low vice, punishable as a crime, but it is now aspiring to respectability, venturing into the open, invading even the drawing rooms of the elegant. Its subtle spread threatens the basis of the economic system and the central principle of personal morality. The only alternative presented to Christian culture here is to fight or to compromise its character.

Ignorance is said to be the mother of devotion. Ignorance

is the mother of nothing—but little ignorances, which grow up to perpetuate and spread the reign of night. The illiteracy of the South Atlantic States is three times as great as that of New England, and more than twice as great as that of the whole country. Our own State is within seven of the bottom of the list of illiteracy. Your responsibility in this field is manifest and urgent. Champion the inalienable rights of the child, play-time and education. Speak the uttermost truth unabashed in the presence of any aristocratic tradition and win the crown which is already made for the most fundamental and constructive of public ministries.

There are other enemies of human life which challenge your Christian culture, the enemies which menace or mar the social order. War is a crime against society. It is deliberate national bankruptcy and suicide. The back of this monster must be broken—you must support the new declaration of war against war, and I now appoint you to commands in the campaign which is already begun. We must break what has been assumed to be the necessary association of war and heroism, reverse our habit of educating every new generation of boys in the military spirit, and extend to national relations the personal code of reason, justice, and law.

The family is the most ancient and important of social institutions. It is menaced by the conditions of modern industry. The sacred bond of marriage appears to be dissolving as the contagion of low moral standards spreads. With the single exception of Japan, our own country has the bad distinction of leading the world in percentage of divorce. I have been authoritatively informed that in an important city of the South-west there is one divorce in every three marriages. What is your intelligence good for if it cannot see the peril of such a tendency? Where, pray, will your Christian impulse express itself, if it build not the breakwater of public conscience and law against this inundation?

The existing economic system is held by many to have grown

up through a succession of blunders. It is certainly now marred by inequality and injustice, which are a standing challenge to every enlightened Christian spirit. What a battlefield is here! You will commit yourself wholeheartedly to the policy which recognizes the downmost man, which enthrones the spirit of fraternity and justice, which softens the conditions under which the poor fight the endless battle for bread, which provides the minimum of necessary working hours under the maximum of wholesome life conditions, which regulates the labor of children and women in the interest of the race, which secures to the workers a fair share in the prosperity which they produce. In short, whatever may be your sphere of action, you will be expected to lead in the reshaping of business and social relations in accordance with the Christian standard.

It must be confessed that organized Christianity is not now recognized in some clearly Christian activities, which on that account are designated not Christian, but humanitarian. To-day when the rising social spirit presents a square challenge to Christianity, some Christian leaders cordially approve, but not a few are actively in the opposition, setting a false alternative and bidding the uninformed choose between theology and sociology, between salvation by grace and salvation by environment. Still others approve with a compromising *but*—approve coldly and briefly, and hasten to warnings which absorb enthusiasm more appropriate to a cordial advocacy. I remind you that the Christian program is not exhausted in the readjustment of any economic system, nor, on the other hand, in insurance against disaster in another world. I cannot agree that the true function of organized religion is correctly described as "that of formulating a man's relations to the mysteries that surround him, and expressing with pomp and poetic emphasis his aspirations toward immortality." In fact, the "pomp and poetic emphasis," at least, appear curiously alien to the meek spirit of its Founder, who went about doing good. Precisely here the need of Christian leadership is called for. For many who are less fortunate than you the social program of Christianity needs to be mediated with tact and intelligence. On the other hand, the serious distinction between Christianity and socialism must be made clear, with the fatal limitation of the socialist program, namely, the impossibility of making a just society out of unjust material. On the other hand, the program of the Kingdom of Heaven must be shown to be all-inclusive, proposing the reconstruction of the social order through the reconstruction of the units which compose it. Here is a task for the Christian layman as well as for the Christian minister.

Some persons refer with apparent pride to their limitations in the appreciation of the beautiful. For example, the old masters are for them not any sort of masters; the great poets are for faddists, they prefer the popinjays of rhyme; the vogue of the higher musical forms, they are quite sure, is an affectation. In the essay on "Inner Beauty," Maeterlinck says that the natural and primitive relationship of soul to soul is a relationship of beauty, beauty is the only language of the soul, in nothing else can the soul take interest. And yet when people come together they appear, out of a strange fear of beauty, to shut the great doors of life and to prefer the baser things wherewith to amuse themselves. If one of such a company have done that day a noble and beautiful thing, he will ascribe it to wretched motives and so relieve himself of its odium. Your introduction here into at least one of the provinces of the realm of beauty will make the apologetic attitude toward any of its forms impossible to you. The essential vulgarity of that feeling needs no further rebuke than the assertion of the place of beauty as an inherent element of the human nature. It is one of the functions of education, but indifferently discharged as yet among us, to lead every growing soul into the racial inheritance of beauty. I am hoping the day will come when art for humanity's sake will find here more distinct recognition in both environment and courses of study. Here again the cultivated youth of this generation may prepare a better day for the next.

The world of politics calls some of you. Do not answer too soon. You will do well to wait upon the ripening of experience before seeking public position. But do not allow the reputed odium of the political career to deter you from a public service which you are able to render. Any career is noble if nobly pursued. The political career is in itself honorable when conceived as "rational experimenting in the light instead of wrangling over the next leap in the dark." Some politicians are like coach-dogs: they follow in front. Their self-seeking may not set the standard of your service. You may not aspire—though I remind you that there is no law against it—you may not aspire, I say, to the distinction of that college man whose enlightened restraint and courage and sanity in the time of world crisis bows the world's heart in deference and gratitude. But in any humbler station where you serve the public need, I charge you, dedicate humbler powers to the same high ends, and like him hold the law of Christ above the tradition of the elders, set up the Christian standard in the market-place, and make the government just and humane, the servant, not the master, of the people.

Whether you do the duties of good citizenship in official or private life, you cannot escape the responsibility of leadership. There will be constructive policies to promote. Coöperation for the common good will require champions. There will be passionate fires to put out, prejudices and superstitions to expose, iniquities entrenched in hoary traditions to dislodge, the weak will need defense, the outcast justice. If the new college man with his chivalry and idealism, his independence and training, fail to respond, what hope can there be of others?

An anonymous but evidently able writer on the problem of reconstructing the present chaotic world order on the basis of adequate knowledge of its factors, says that his design is merely "to give a little twist in the right direction to one or other of the giant intellects which are possibly, and even probably, ripening around us." None of you may be ripening into the Aristotle of this great synthesis, but I confidently expect you to hold commissions of varying responsibility under him. It is the vastness of the world that hinders us from reducing its chaos to a humane and rational order. You may assist in the analysis of the problem, you may contribute an organizing principle in one section of life, you may enlist or train the recruits of the new order, you may mold the public mind to the pattern of the mind of Christ, you may marshal the forces of justice and light against the oppressor who darkens counsel to cover up injustice. Whatever your special task may be in the growing good of the world, your position will be one of leadership. That leadership you will consider not a prize, but a burden, not so much a distinction as an opportunity. But the more unselfishly it is undertaken, the more certainly will the burden become a prize and the opportunity a distinction. Permit me at once to warn and to encourage you with the great principle of Christ, that the height of the pyramid of distinction will be in direct proportion to the area of the base of service.

THE KNIGHT-ERRANTRY OF MEDICINE*

1916

> The degree of estimation in which any profession is held becomes the standard of the estimation in which the professors hold themselves.—*Burke, Reflections.*

In one of Conan Doyle's vivid stories of adventure a young man's advances receive a chilling response. His Juliet explains that he has done nothing to win her admiration, nothing heroic to fire her imagination. "But," he urges, "I will when opportunity comes." She replies: "There are heroisms all around us waiting to be done, and a woman's heart is the reward of the man who will do them." He had presently his perilous adventure in recovering to science "the lost world" of the Jurassic period surviving on a plateau beyond the head waters of the Amazon, and returned to find that he had lost his prize to a commonplace scrap of a man; but the enrichment of his nature and its developed heroism were his forever. The calling on which you shortly enter is in its history and nature heroic, and if you are worthy of it, whether you win or lose its incidental prizes of pelf and contemporary reputation, you will participate in its nobleness and bless yourself with the heroism which you sought to promote. You will illustrate in the twentieth century the chivalry of the thirteenth, and amid the sordid economics and materialism of the time establish "the manly sentiment and heroic enterprise" of the great day when knighthood was in flower. Such considerations lead me to suggest for our topic "The Knight-Errantry of Medicine."

The martial ideal is written deep in the human constitution by millenniums of battle. In the Crusades, to the strength of

---

* Address to the Graduating Class of the Virginia College of Medicine, Richmond, June 6, 1916.

heredity it added the consecration of religion.   The war tradition of Southern Europe and the war tradition of the barbarian North met one another at the threshold of the Christian Church, were invited in, and there followed the unnatural alliance of Christ and Mars.   The knight was the embodiment of this composite ideal, and rode forth, as did the Knights Templar, pledged "to fight with a pure mind for the supreme and true King."   The Templars were from the first a military order. The Knights of St. John, or Hospitallers, were originally a nursing brotherhood, which developed in connection with a Jerusalem hospital for pilgrims, and only later took on the military habit and function.   The third order of knights which sprang out of the Crusades is likewise associated with a hospital in Jerusalem.   Near the close of the twelfth century certain German merchants established in a ship drawn ashore at Acre a rude hospital which was afterwards transferred to the Holy City and attached to the German Church of St. Mary the Virgin.   Like the Hospitallers, the Teutonic Knights gradually assumed the military rôle, but both these orders of knighthood throughout their history recognized their chief obligation to be to care for the sick.

That mixed system of opinion and sentiment, to use Burke's noble phrases, that generous loyalty to rank and sex, that sensibility of principle, that chastity of honor which felt a stain like a wound, which ennobled whatever it touched and under which vice itself lost half its evil by losing all its grossness—the glory of Europe, chivalry, found its proper expression in the orders of the knights.   Espousing the cause of the weak and the outcast, the knights were under the severest bonds to noble and chivalrous conduct.

> And one there was among us, ever moved
> Among us in white armor, Galahad.
> "God make thee good as thou art beautiful,"
> Said Arthur, when he dubbed him knight.

The knight-errant was a wandering knight who rode abroad

redressing human wrongs, devoting "the unbought grace of life," the skill and prowess of hand to the protection and succor of the defenseless. Knight-errantry, of course, was the knightly practice of seeking heroic adventures under the high law which subordinates one's total equipment to the public or private exigency.

Now, medicine is the field of a genuine knight-errantry. The stages of its historical development have been marked by knightly adventures which risked all in the service of human need. From Hippocrates to Wright and Flexner, through privation and calumny, in loneliness and persecution and exhausting labors, these knights of medicine have struggled through a horror of great darkness to answer the cry of distress. They have been themselves broken on the wheel of fortune; but the reign of night has been broken also. Diseases which decimated the race are under control, the mortality of many others is greatly reduced, and the average duration of human life extended nearly threefold.

Consider an example or two of the later time. The exploits and adventures of the new medicine are worthy of standing with those of the Christian missionary enterprise. In the Pasteur Institute a little body of scientists have surrendered the ambitions and interests of ordinary men and, sharing their goods, live in austere devotion to the common purpose of extending the boundaries of human knowledge. "Rumors of war and peace, echoes of the turmoil of politics and religion, pass unheeded over their monastic seclusion; but if there come news of a strange disease in China or Peru, a scientific emissary is ready with his microscope and his tubes to serve as a missionary of the new knowledge and the new hope that Pasteur has brought to suffering humanity." Similar brotherhoods, in those sacred temples where devotion and skill are saying ever and anon of the victim of disease, "Loose him and let him go!" laboratories like the Institute of Tropical Medicine in Liverpool and the Rockefeller Institute of Medical Research

in New York, send out the knights of the new order to check
typhus in Serbia, to solve the mystery and break the tyranny
of sleeping-sickness in Uganda, to dig the Panama Canal with
the extracted drills and suckers of Stegomyia Fasciata, to ex-
terminate hookworm in an anæmic belt around the globe.

And there in an immortal niche stands Nathaniel Hodges of
London, who in 1665 was the first man to do a post-mortem
on a plague patient. And here is Louis Pasteur leaning over
the head of a bulldog with bloodshot eyes and body convulsed
with spasms. He is sucking up into a tube some drops of
saliva at the distance of a finger's length from the foaming
head—and you know the result. While he was engrossed with
the study of splenic fever, Pasteur came to have what his daughter calls the face of an approaching discovery. If he was timidly
asked what stage the investigation had reached, he would reply,
"I can tell you nothing. I dare not express aloud what I
hope." One day he came up from his laboratory with the
face of triumph. Tears of joy were in his eyes. As he em-
braced the members of his family, he said, "I should never
console myself if such a discovery as my assistants and I have
just made were not a French discovery."

See young Bruce and his heroic wife driving an ox-team
through swarms of deadly tsetse flies into the heart of Zulu-
land to open Africa to the white man.

You will recall the brilliant research of Surgeon Walter Reed
on the etiology of yellow fever. He went in true knightly spirit
into the peril of the smitten region with a body of equally
noble associates determined to find the cause of the dreadful
malady. Among them was Dr. James Carroll, who submitted
to the bite of an infected mosquito, in four days was ill with a
severe attack of yellow fever, and demonstrated the agent of
its spread. He recovered, but with impaired health, and died
in 1907 of an affection of the heart which resulted from that
heroic experiment.

In 1888 a friend said to me in the Apennine Mountains that

I need not hesitate to make a summer visit to Rome if I should take against Roman fever the simple precaution of putting down my windows at 5 p.m. to exclude the night air. The precaution was really effective, but the explanation was erroneous. The night air did not do the mischief, but the Anopheles which floated in on it; reminding one of the Shakespearean prescription of a pinch of mummy dust in hot water for a certain affection. Any other dust or no dust in hot water would have served as well. On the basis of the observations of Laveran (1880), of Manson (1894), and of Ross (1895), Dr. Sambon and Dr. Low of the London School of Tropical Medicine went in 1900 to reside in one of the most dangerous districts of the Roman Campagna in the most dangerous season of the year, using only the precaution of confining themselves between sunset and sunrise to their mosquito-proof dwelling. During the same season eight Red Cross ambulances, each with a doctor and attendant, went into the deadly Campagna. These experiments, with others of like heroic quality, established the mosquito-parasitic theory of malaria, and wrote for mankind a new declaration of independence.

The beloved physician of Saranac Lake, himself on the verge of the White Plague precipice, saved thousands from its insatiable abyss, turning them back to the smiling plains of health, and unconscious of his heroism and power, as he was of the magnitude of his task, led a forelorn hope to realization. The name of Edward Livingston Trudeau shows fair and bright on the roster of the knight-errantry of medicine. Referring in 1908 to the thirty monkeys used in the discovery of the serum for the cure of cerebro-spinal meningitis, Dr. Simon Flexner said: "If I could be assured that a cure for tuberculosis would be the result, I would gladly be one of thirty men to sacrifice my life for such a discovery. What is more, the other twenty-nine would be forthcoming; there would be plenty of volunteers."

Into such a noble fellowship you pass tonight. This is the

knighthood of medicine, and you are now come to your consecration hour. Whether you devote yourself to research or to personal ministry, the vows of the medical chivalry will be upon you, the lofty ideal of an adventurous, self-sacrificing heroism will shine before you and save you, let us hope, from the meanness and trickery of the competitive private tradesman selling pedantry and colored water, and hold you true to the finest traditions of your profession.

But I should be unfaithful if I did not remind you of that knight-errant of Old Spain, Don Quixote. His heated imagination, you remember, turned wayside inns into armed castles, the hammer strokes of a fuller's mill into the thunders of waters precipitated from the high mountains of the moon, forty windmills into as many giants waving defiant arms; and, with grandiloquent speeches and the manner of a lofty heroism, he mounted his bony Rosinante and resolutely charged them all. Cervantes, whose tercentenary coincides precisely with that of Shakespeare, in this romance of Don Quixote laughed knight-errantry out of respectability. Even so your profession, in spite of its lofty ideals and its wide ranging beneficence has been made to contribute to the mirth of nations. And it has been attacked directly on one flank or another—its vivisections, its inoculations, its mercenary practice—more than once with a serious ferocity quite calculated to befuddle, if not control, a considerable section of the laity.

For example, Pliny of the first century hated doctors and justified his antipathy in part by declaring in his *Natural History* that Rome got on without them for six hundred years. Julius Cæsar is said to have given foreign doctors—there were no native—the freedom of the city to attract them; but the successors of such as came seem to have been officially banished about 200 A.D. And you will recall that seventeenth century comedy, Molière's *The Doctor in Spite of Himself*. With a well-oiled tongue and a resourcefulness which is unembarrassed by any moral restraints, this unwilling doctor explains his patient's dumbness as due to "the acrimony of the humors engendered in the concavity of the diaphragm," and, going into some detail, places the liver on the left side and the heart on the right.   When called to task on his anatomy, he replies that those organs were, indeed, differently located in former times ; "but we have altered all that, and we now practice medicine in quite a new way."   There is Maarten Maartens' scathing attack on medical practice in his novel, *The New Religion*.   Bernard Shaw's five-act drama, *The Doctor's Dilemma*, of 1906, is preceded by a ninety-two page preface in which argument, satire, ridicule, and an amazing knowledge of technical matters appear to leave little room for the profession as a private calling.   He would municipalize Harley Street.   He would have the private operator treated as a private executioner ought to be treated, and persons professing to cure disease, as fortune-tellers.   He would compel a doctor to inscribe in his doorplate the words, "Remember that I, too, am mortal."   Beside these critics of distinction there are individuals here and there who do not hesitate to avow a want of confidence in the reliability and usefulness of the profession.   I may remark, however, that such persons are apt, in spite of their theories, to send for the doctor when they fall into trouble.

Is there any explanation of the criticism which I have briefly illustrated?   Much of it is serious and deserves attention.

One thing seems clear.   Just as the individual knight gave the satirist his opportunity against knighthood, so the individual doctor gives the critic his opportunity against medicine.   It is the foibles and follies of particular doctors here and there that discredit the profession.   It survives in respectability in spite of them.   Some of these lapses from standard may be mentioned with profit : the grand manner, the air of condescension with everybody who is not a doctor ; impossible claims ; discrimination in service on the basis of financial returns ; professional jealousies, in which doctors appear to enjoy an odious monopoly; disagreement in advice to the same patient—one doctor, "You don't eat enough fish"; his colleague, "A fish diet will give you leprosy"; one, "A restricted diet—stomach needs rest"; his colleague, "Eat what you want and when you want it"; parading technical terms as if "they do not really understand what they are trying to say and so cannot find familiar words for it," reminding one of the old Irish tale of a bard whose speech before the king and his warriors was warmly praised because neither the king nor any other could understand him, "so great was his high, noble, beautiful obscurity"; oracular instruction in details which nature has provided for in organized instincts, as how to love, how to eat, how to breathe—illustrated by James Lane Allen's picture of a wise old sheep, Dr. Buck, giving a lecture on breathing to a flock of spring lambs. Against all such invasions of the integrity of your noble calling I should be glad to give every man of you stiff, undiluted, oft-repeated inoculations of the vaccine of common sense; and I am not sure that I should wait upon the suggestion of the opsonic index.

And now, gentlemen, as I conclude, permit me to remind you that the opportunities for heroic adventure are not all in the past. Such as have been cited from the unfolding history of medicine are meant, in fact, merely to present the spirit in which you are to meet those now but a little way ahead of you. That old dragon, Disease, has not yet been killed. With poisonous breath he is still spreading irremediable suffering, defects, and death throughout every generation of little children, which is God's fresh and undiscouraged effort to save the world. The tender shoots of life he will blight from afar, reaching them through a tainted heredity; and you must strike him there, if at all. You will meet him intrenched behind corporate indifference. You will meet him in many an uncompanioned struggle through slow night hours, with no witnesses but God, on whom patient and doctor alike must rely.

In the shadows just beyond these bright precincts another

dragon waits to challenge your knight-errantry. His name is
Superstition. Whether we like it or do not like it, ghosts still
walk, although it is broad day. Here is madam rising in horror from her generous board when she discovers that the company numbers precisely thirteen. There are gentlemen of
general intelligence who carry on their persons one sort of
amulet or another to insure good luck or to ward off disease.
A lady within sound of college bells refused on the first of
January to admit her cook to prepare breakfast because it fore-
boded evil if a woman was the first to enter the house on New
Year's day. One thinks of Sam Jones' recognition of degrees
of ignorance—ignorance and ignor*ance*. These illustrations are
of the last order and degree. But I am thinking of current
superstitions about disease. There is the fundamental and
palpable delusion underlying Christian Science. There is the
soft, undiscriminating sentimentalism which sobs convulsively
over little Fido, with never a thought for Fido's little mistress
choking with diphtheria.   Is not the suspicious awe with which
the insane and the epileptic are still regarded a survival of the
mediaeval superstition that they were possessed by the devil?
And how shall we account for the inadequate provision for the
care and cure of the insane except on the view that the public
stands still in need of some degrees more of enlightenment
and humanity? Think of committing the victim of some brain
disorder to the neglect and odium of the common jail! Probably the most widespread of these superstitions is that which
regards disease of any sort as the toll which Providence exacts
for sin, and mortality statistics as the record of the decrees of
God. Will you take up this dragon's challenge?

Another struggle awaits you, and I mention it here because
you are men first and doctors afterwards. Your human obligations are primary, your medical secondary. In fact, medical
obligations are binding only in so far as they are human. I
refer to your struggle with an ignorant conservatism which
stands right athwart the path to coöperative action for the

common good in public hygiene, and with which vested interests are in close alliance. When conservatism gives over the fight, vested interests may be counted upon to renew it. If you find yourself in need of inspiration, look at the public sanitation work of Dr. Watson Rankin of North Carolina and Dr. Oscar Dowling of Louisiana. Society is in a lower stage of development than the men who compose it. The State is not so good or so efficient as its citizens are; the Church is not so true to the Christian ideal as are its members. Individually, Americans are efficient; collectively, timid. You will be called on to lead in a campaign to make yourselves superfluous, to bring the organized forces of society to fight disease and vice as the social units now fight them. You will fight the indifference of the Government, which spends less than 2 per cent of the National income on these fundamental and ever-present perils and 83 per cent on army and navy to defend us from an enemy which it cannot name. And the jingoism and hysteria of the present moment will carry this extravagant expenditure to a much higher figure.

But there is no need of further specification. I am content if you have caught a glimpse of the heroic ministry which is before you and discovered perhaps descending upon you anew the knightly spirit and ideal of your great profession. To have been noble once obliges us to be noble ever afterward, and to be stationed in a succession of heroism obliges us to perpetuate it. You take your place tonight in the goodly fellowship "of the invincible knights of old." Let that fellowship be henceforth at once your safety and your inspiration.

CULTURE AND PATRIOTISM

1916

The Hebrew had a narrow view of the richness of life, its variety and beauty; for the second Commandment slew idolatry and art together. The delicacies of perception on which art depends were not his. The genial sympathies which warm up under contemplation of the beauty of the world were for him chilled at their source, and natural grace expressing itself in varied aesthetic forms, as in the Greek, was restrained and silenced before the Hebrew's consciousness of God. And so there is no Hebrew head of Yahweh over against the Greek head of Zeus in the temple of art, but the lofty conception of God robed in light and girded with righteousness makes ample compensation. He need not be an artist, who supplies the material and inspiration of art. The Hebrew genius blossomed in religion, and religion is the soul of art. There the Hebrew touches humanity at its highest point, there he still teaches and guides us, and it is he who prompts our faltering speech whenever we stand face to face with God.

Another distinction of this marvellously gifted people hardly less striking is its racial integrity. The conquest of Canaan welded the tribes of Israel into a nation. From the life of wilderness Bedouin they passed into the settled life of farmers. They grew wheat and grapes and olives and lived in villages and towns. The Exile destroyed the nation. The people were scattered over the world from Cappadocia to Egypt, from Rome to Chaldea. They became traders, and, in spite of their wide dispersion, they retained their racial unity by the most powerful of all social bonds, the bond of a common religion. Their leaders recognized the peril of losing racial identity, of sinking into the mass of the peoples who showed them hospitality and permitted their occupations. Accordingly, they revived the Mosaic code regulating the life of the Chosen Peo-

ple in foreign lands. In every Jewish community the syna-
gogue, the house of prayer and preaching, sprang up to meet
the need of instruction in these laws. And so these patriots
without a country developed the institutions and interests
which mark them today, and preserved and consolidated, under the sanction of religion, a racial integrity which is hardly
paralleled in all history.

Psalm 137, which I read to you, is an example of the only
form of beauty in which the Hebrew excelled, the lyric. That
Psalm is a lyric of patriotism. It is not alone in our collection.
Psalm 122 is hardly less ardent and beautiful: "Pray for the
peace of Jerusalem. They shall prosper that love thee. Peace
be within thy walls and prosperity within thy palaces." And
the 87th belongs in this lovely patriotic fellowship. The widely
scattered Jews still hold Jerusalem to be their common mother:
"Of Zion it shall be said this one and that one was born in her.
All my fountains are in thee." To the intense patriotism of
these Psalms the 137th adds the element of exclusiveness. It
is of the early Babylonian captivity. Ten thousand nobles,
soldiers, and artisans of Judea, deported by Nebuchadnezzar,
cultivated their own lands on a large irrigation canal to the
south of Babylon, under some sort of local government, and
enjoying some degree of prosperity. Now and again they remember Zion and weep. Our poet pictures a forlorn group
of the exiles, required to sing a song of their native land, silent
as the harps which they have hung on the willows of the great
river, and then, on his own behalf, he breaks out into a rhap-
sody which has been the classic utterance of patriotism for all
succeeding time:

> If I forget thee, O Jerusalem,
> Let my right hand forget her skill.
> Let my tongue cleave to the roof of my mouth,
> If I remember thee not;
> If I prefer not Jerusalem
> Above my chief joy.

But his ardor sweeps him on into an exclusive and bitter attitude toward other peoples. Attachment to Jerusalem involves hatred of all its enemies. Edom and Babylon are singled out each for a special vengeance. The sons of Edom had rejoiced over the calamity of Jerusalem, saying of the fated city, "Clean down, down to the ground with it!" and the poet prays that some day that account may be squared. Babylon had accomplished the devastation which had delighted Edom, and the patriot poet sings the praises of the man who will devastate Babylon in requital and, seizing her little children, dash them to pieces against a rock.

This general attitude was shared by Ezekiel, the most distinguished member of that Hebrew colony on the Euphrates. A vigorous and impressive thinker, he counseled submission to Babylon. He was broad-minded enough to recognize the sin and judgment of his native land, but he was unable to think of any other land except as either a servant or an enemy of his own. He praises Babylon in spite of its immorality because he believes it to be the divine instrument to secure the ultimate prosperity of Israel. Against Ammon, Moab, Edom, Philistia, Tyre, Sidon, and Egypt he puts in Yahweh's mouth the bitterest of invectives, because he believes them to be the enemies of Israel. God has chosen Israel for Israel's sake; other nations must be crushed into subordination or extinction.

A greater prophet than Ezekiel proclaimed a different philosophy of history. Isaiah, who in this matter was in accord with Paul of the later time, held that Israel was chosen, not for Israel's sake, but for the sake of other nations, chosen to be the purveyor of religious truth to the whole world: Israel for the world, not the world for Israel.

I am bringing before you today in so much of detail these national attachments and repulsions of the ancient Hebrew world precisely because they are neither ancient nor Hebrew, in the sense of being restricted in period or race. They are, rather, timeless and human. They have never been without historical illustration; but, embodying as they do objectively and with such accuracy the national feelings of the present moment, they may exhibit to us instructively our own disguised attitudes and direct us as we now inquire into the existing world situation and the college graduate's relation to it. You are completing your college training in a period of intense nationalism, before which treaties are but "scraps of paper" and international law slowly built up through three hundred years of intercourse and discussion appears to be all but bankrupt. The occasion provides the theme, "Culture and Patriotism."

Patriotism is, of course, love of one's country. It is a sentiment of loyalty which on occasion expresses itself in practical service to the country, defending its territory and its rights from invasion, maintaining its name and order and institutions. Under its influence men regard their country as an organic whole and identify themselves with its fortunes. They feel it to be a unity, not an aggregate of sections. To an American patriot, for example, a northern economic success is a national success, a southern problem is a national responsibility. If King Lynch mounts anarchy and rides out to murder in any State, all the rest bow in a common shame. When Spain outrages the national conscience, Californian and New Yorker, Michigander and Carolinian, vie with one another in the liberation of the oppressed. When Japan touches the country's nerve at the Golden Gate, the response is prompt and deep all the way to Hatteras and Boston Harbor.

An eminent English political writer held love of one's country to be a lesson of reason, not an institution of nature; a precept of morality, not an instinct or principle of passion. I venture to disagree. It is, rather, a primary, unreasoning loyalty. Reason may confound but not shake its devotion. As Chesterton puts the matter, we belong to our country before we begin to ask if it is nice to belong to it; we find ourselves fighting for the flag before we have ever enlisted. In another place he complains that Kipling admires England, but does not love her, for we admire things with reasons, but love them without reason. National loyalty, like personal loyalty, is deeper in our nature than admiration and is already compromised when it seeks to justify itself. And, like the ancient Hebrew patriotism, it lapses easily into exclusiveness and inhospitality.

Mr. Wells, even in the act of asserting his own detachment from the common delusion that one's country is superior to all others, is compelled to admit that he is gratified by flattering falsehoods about English superiority, that he is ever ready to believe that the scenery, poetry, and even the music of England is in some mystic and impregnable way the best. Balzac finds it easy to explain the English inclination and the French reluctance to travel. "Something better than England," says he, "is everywhere to be found : whereas it is excessively difficult to find the charms of France outside of France." And here is Dollinger insisting that Germany is the intellectual center of the ideas that sway the world ; no other nation can approach the Germans in manysidedness, in the power of adaptation, and in the qualities of untiring research and original creative genius. And, not to be outdone in this competition of the heart's extravagance and partiality, up comes our own Dr. Josiah Strong. "Ours is the elect nation," he affirms. "We are taller and heavier and live longer than other men ; we are richer and more energetic, of finer nervous organization"—ticketing, as an English competitor says derisively, ticketing neurasthenia as the fine susceptibility of genius. And Ireland, the nation without a flag, that "little bit of heaven which fell from out the sky one day"—you recall what the Irishman said of it when he and an American and a Scotchman were asked what would be their second choice of a nationality. Jonathan and Sandy would deplore the necessity of such a choice but agreed upon England as the alternative. "Pat," said the inquisitor, "if you were not an Irishman, what would you be?" "Faith," he replied, "an' I'd be ashamed of meself!"

The sentiment of patriotic loyalty which I have sought to illustrate is quickened by national disaster, and in time of international collision and crisis it may be fanned up into a veritable frenzy, when a question becomes an impertinence, deliberation cowardice, and the voice of wisdom the instrument of treachery.

Permit me to raise a question with you today. You and the 40,000 American college graduates of this season were born in the atmosphere of patriotism, and the years of your own unfolding life coincide with your country's most rapid and important development in international relations. Its position today is unique and splendid. The chivalrous adventure in behalf of Cuba in '98, the all but sudden recognition of international obligations which followed, and the direct and sane and righteous diplomacy initiated by John Hay brought the United States with marvelous rapidity into a position of leadership and responsibility quite beyond the dreams and desires of the founders of our national polity. But I fancy that, if those gray and reverend shades are now as alert as once they were to the weal of the Republic, they must be pleased and expectant. Jealous as Washington was of European influence in American counsels, earnest as was his warning against permanent alliances with any portion of the foreign world, he cannot discover in the new relations of the present hour any abatement of the national spirit, any compromise of our national solidarity. Whether we wish it or do not wish it, the conditions of modern life make national isolation impossible. The expanding network of international commercial relations involves international political relations. However matters stood in the past, certainly today no nation liveth unto itself—a truth taught us in unforgettable symbols by that horrible and wicked business which stretches a red hand 3,000 miles over seas to disturb our peace and reverse the policies of a hundred years. We have, indeed, seen a notable quickening of national spirit. You have yourselves participated in it. The world situation has played up the attractions of our country, and she makes now an unwonted appeal to our enthusiasm and devotion. And you, I know, respond. My question is, what sort of response do you make? Students of Princeton and Harvard and Yale and other institutions are enlisting for military training. With that sort of response I am not now concerned. It is probably in no way different from the response of young men who have not had the opportunity of college training. I am asking, rather, what is the college man's attitude toward all the factors of nationalism, what is the reaction of culture in the new world of jostling sovereignties into which you now pass?

Culture presents many aspects. It may be recognized as the sum of the dominant interests, tastes, and appreciations, the climate of sentiment and opinion, of a particular community; or a certain gentility and poise and ease of movement amid the refinements of social intercourse; or that richness of the inner personal life which shares and reflects the moral and intellectual wealth of the ages. I am thinking of it now in yet another aspect. A keen writer of the time describes barbarism as being incapable of reciprocity, and sets down a certain highly civilized people as barbarians because they have no little mirrors in their minds in which to see the minds of other men. Let us think of culture as the opposite of that kind of barbarism, as a tolerance and sympathy which are the fruit of knowledge of men and things. Culture in this sense is another name for horizon.

Four factors of the national life confront this culture today with a sharp insistence—individualism, provincialism, nationalism, and humanism. Consider individualism first.

As individuals Americans are practical and efficient in industrial enterprises, but as a nation they are incompetent, permitting industrial anarchy and waste out of consideration tion for private initiative. Individuals exercise a gracious ministry to the needy and suffering, but the State looks down on the tragedy of the underworld, where the down-and-outs fight

for breath and bread, and beats them back to maintain a
theory! We are individually progressive, but collectively
timid. All which indicates that society is in a lower stage of
development than the men who compose it, that the State is
not so good or efficient as its citizens.

What is the reaction of culture to such a situation? It demands that this social incompetence and drift be mastered and
guided, that neither academic theories nor tradition shall stand
in the way of social beneficence and social justice. It teaches
that, as individualism in religion is selfishness and in finance
miserliness, so individualism in politics is anarchy. Society is
possible only on the principle of its supremacy. Community
interest is paramount to individual interest. Advancement in
civilization is, indeed, measurable by the restrictions which
society imposes upon its members for the sake of the general
welfare. You may not carry in your own pocket a pistol
bought with your own money. You may not spit on the side-
walk. You may not sell another the whiskey which you own
and he wants. Such limitations of personal liberty are not
found in backward stages of civilization. If imposed by an
external authority they would be intolerable, but imposed by
the common will for the common good, they become the symbols of a genuine freedom. You, gentlemen, as the exponents
of the culture of which I speak, will do no finer thing than
pushing forward the consciousness of the community life where
alone individual life finds completeness, the consciousness of
our social solidarity. For such a developed consciousness, together with a common enlightenment, is our salvation from
the perils inherent in democracy.

Provincialism need not detain us. It is a certain local emphasis of thought and interest which is at once obnoxious to
culture and an obstruction in the path of national development. It results in a motley code of laws within the boundaries of a single State—"Except my county!" cries the local
patriot in the General Assembly—and in the country at large

national issues must bow to State's rights, and even yet the tongue of the average congressman can frame to pronounce "my district" a little better than "my country." But allow me to warn you that your patriotism, if it is sincere, will root itself in the community where you live. Your national patriotism is the extension of a genuine local patriotism. It certainly finds at home its concrete expression. Most of us will serve our country best by serving our town.

Nationalism is national spirit, national devotion. It is another name for patriotism. Its characteristics have been already indicated. I recall it here to point out the peril of its extreme development. The patriotic bias is forgivable. It is more: it is wholesome and beautiful. Let Englishman, Frenchman, German, American, say with William Watson, each of his own country—

> O England, shouldst thou one day fall,
> Justice were weaker throughout all
> The world, and truth less passionately free,
> And God the poorer for thine overthrow!

But nationalism must be chastened by culture lest it become exclusive and bumptious, arrogant and full of hate. Its marked development during the past century has been at some expense of "the cosmopolitan sense of human relations," and just at the monent when, through business intercourse and the applications of science, the world had become a neighborhood and was about to become a brotherhood, this excessive nationalism hurled the competing sovereignties of Europe against one another, and the folly and tragedy of 1914 fell. That lurid tragedy has wrecked civilization from the Baltic to the Aegean and threatens to seize humanity itself, palpitating and helpless, in its bloody clutches. And America shows signs of infection in a rising temperature of national spirit. What is the obligation of the cultivated man at such a moment? Not to be less loyal, but more generous. Not to strangle his nationalism, but to cool it down with humanism. Lord Nelson said that the mark of a true Englishman was to hate a Frenchman like the devil. How would that sound in the comradeship of heroism in the trenches of Flanders? The cultivated man knows that the sovereign gifts of the human spirit have been widely and somewhat evenly distributed, that nations educate one another, and that each has made its contribution of value to the common civilization. How poor that civilization would be without the equality and radiance of France, the science and organization of Germany, the art of Italy, the epic mystery of Russia, the immortal literature of England, the dignity of India, the reverence of China, and "the smiling heroism of Japan." Into American life all these streams flow as nowhere else, making it rich and cosmopolitan. Surely the American college man, if any man, will love his country, but remember the sources of its manifold wealth. He will insist upon her rights, but recognize her debts. He will respond in patriotism to her appeal, but he will not put patriotism before justice, nor violate the rights of humanity.

Permit me to remind you of the symbolism and legend of the seal of your college. This is its declaration : Christ is the light of the world, and Wake Forest College is an agent of its dissemination for the benefit of mankind. You are committed. The vows of American citizenship are upon you, but also those of the universal Kingdom of God. The illumination of your Christian culture is not for you, but for others, and its quality is tested by the range of its regard. It will show you opportunities of coöperative service with your neighbors, but it will find you brothers over every great circle of the globe. Your tasks will be local, but your interests planetary. You will be attached at home, but you will be "public and human." *Humanitas pro humanitate.* To such a spirit and habit of mind, how alien the prejudice bred by ignorance, the social gulfs fixed, class hatreds, international jealousies ; how trivial the considerations for which diplomats labor, intrigue, and finally fly at one another's throats! How true and obedient is such an attitude to the spirit and mind of our Lord, who said, "Other sheep I have which are not of this fold."

CULTURE AND KULTUR

1917

Nowhere in America at this pregnant and fateful hour can any man speak to any audience except in the atmosphere of patriotism, least of all to an audience of young men fresh from the baptism of consecration to their country's ultimate demand. Some places in your ranks are vacant. Your fellows are absent, but accounted for. The pressure of a particular form of service required haste and they ran to meet it. The forms of service upon which you will enter none the less heartily, none the less nobly, may be even more vital in the present emergency, for they will equip the nation for its chivalrous adventure, preserve its civil life from disruption, and make ready the path of its greater destiny when the sun comes out after the storm to bless an abiding peace in righteousness. The suggestion of the situation is compelling. I speak to you of "Culture and Kultur."

The greatest German scholar and scientist of the nineteenth century visited Professor Hugo Münsterberg in Cambridge. He was shown the magnificent equipment of Harvard, its scientific institutes and laboratories, but was told that these were not the true America. The true America was not a place and could be understood only by entering with sympathy into the deeper invisible powers at the bottom of the national soul. Hemholtz leaned back in his chair a long time. "Then," says Professor Münsterberg, "he looked at me with his marvelous great eyes and said quietly, 'You have a great task before you, if you really want to reach the mind of Europe with that message'." The eminent psychologist had, indeed, set himself the task of interpreting America to Germany and Germany to America, but when he died the task was so far from being accomplished that the reciprocal obscurity had become a clear and acute antagonism, ripened now into irreconcilable collision.

[86]

The development of these opposing national ideals, as is the case in many widely divergent organic forms, pursued in its earlier stages the same path. It is a long and bloody road up which the race has blundered and fought from the jungle to Washington and Berlin, Paris and Vienna. Traffic on this highway is still open, and ever and anon a jungle instinct, like a night robber, springs out at the throat of civilization and threatens to drag it back to the elemental passions and brutality of its wild past. Jungle plunder still clutters the path of our progress and jungle ways compromise the claims of our culture. But slow and painful as the rise of the Western World out of savagery has been, and insecure as its latest advances appear, there can be no question of its real advance or of the common path which all sections of it have taken for the greater part of the journey. Practically the whole of Europe has participated in the progressive legislation which has softened the conditions of human life within each independent national unit. This legislation has been described as a continuous series of concessions by the power-holding class to the underprivileged masses. Under what pressure have these concessions been made? Under the pressure of a body of opinion and feeling intolerant of suffering and wrong. It stiffens the demand of the masses and at the same time disintegrates the resistance of the governing class until a revolution is precipitated, and a new stage of social development begins. A number of factors may be involved, as the spread of intelligence, the ease of communication, the organization of industry, but they may all be traced to one root—the growth of humanitarian sentiments, the softening and refining of character, which are the most notable mark of Christian civilization. Lord Bryce has taught us that it is on the religious life that nations repose. No less certainly does the progress of Western society get its impulse and direction from "the fund of altruism with which Christianity equipped it in its cradle." Western culture is Christian culture.

I beg to remind you that there has been a slower but parallel development in the relations of independent nationalities to one another. The separate states with which the modern world began in the sixteenth century were sovereign, each the source of the only law it recognized. Machiavelli, the powerful and unscrupulous Machiavelli, was their prophet. He proclaimed their emancipation from all moral restraints, and based international relations on military force alone. There were protests here and there. Before the close of the sixteenth century it was boldly affirmed that the conduct of states should be controlled by legal rules. Grotius, the father of international law, made in the seventeenth century the first impressive appeal to the moral motive in state action. And we must not forget that the laws of chivalry expressed very nobly the Christian principle of universal humanity and constituted the moral basis of the military traditions of Europe. These traditions found latest and fullest development in the specific conventions of the Hague Conferences and involve the fundamental principles of international law as it is conceived today, namely, fidelity to a promise, honesty in the means employed for injuring an enemy, restriction of the areas and suffering of war, respect and protection towards the weak. In short, international law is the practical application of the teaching of Jesus in the field of international relations.

I have sketched the main line of the development of individual and national morality. Until now we have thought it the only line. It has required the tragedy and horror of the Great War to teach us better. We have discovered a divergent line of evolution upon an opposite principle, and the shock of that discovery still vibrates round the world. The divergence from the normal development may be distinctly seen in the world of politics in the legacy which Frederick the Great left the later rulers of Prussia—the tradition that success justifies everything and that moral scruples are proofs of contemptible weakness if they imperil success. In the sphere of philosophy Kant taught that the individual life finds completeness only in the associative life. Hegel conceived the state as the largest and noblest form of the associative life and its mandate and necessity, therefore, as absolutely supreme. Treitschke interpreted history in conformity with this conception, and Bismarck and William II have made history so. Austria was forced into war in 1866, France in 1870, the world in 1914. If treaties stand in the way of national ambition, they become scraps of paper. If the wounded writhe inconveniently, they are bayoneted, even when they are German. If the ship is unarmed and gay on the laughing seas with women and children, down she dives with a hole in her ribs to terrorize the careless. If the demon of the undersea bats the water out of his one eye and glimpses a food ship or a hospital ship, he launches his fatal dart and settles to the safe depths chuckling over another victim of the supremacy of the state. Art treasures which are the best wealth of the world are destroyed ruthlessly, non-combatant populations are deported, fruitful regions left uninhabitable, nameless outrages authorized, the hard-won victories of decency, humanity, and democracy menaced with utter annihilation—this gentlemen, is Prussian "blood and iron" pressed through to its bitter issue; this is the practical fruit of the German theory that the state— the German State—is above all law and is called of God to dominate the world. This theory is the heart of German Kultur. It is a purely intellectual development for purely economic and political reasons. It has been sedulously inculcated by the powerful apparatus of the state system of education and is now a positive obsession of one of the noblest and most gifted of races. This obsession must be dislodged, this national waywardness corrected. It is in square conflict with the Christian culture for which this institution stands. It is at close grips with the democracy, humanity, and justice for which our great country stands. You take up the responsibilities of cultured manhood and pass out of college directly into this struggle. It is the greatest moment of modern history. The contending forces are the most gigantic, the stake the biggest over which the iron dice of war ever rattled. To be provincial or self-centered now is to be doubly base. To be cold now when the tides of moral indignation are surging in the universal human heart and cleansing it of littleness, is to be inhuman. To be pessimistic now when God is mobilizing the forces of righteousness and freedom against an arrogant autocracy and sketching before our eyes the outlines of the Kingdom of Heaven, is to despair of mankind and lose faith in Him.

CULTURE AND CRISIS

1918

In 1914 the impossible happened. We relied on a number of considerations in our judgment that there could be no world war. Preparation for war was so widespread and so complete that we fondly fancied no nation would risk a collision with any of its neighbors. Economic relations were so intimate and universal that a disruption in one section would be so disastrous to all sections that the world of business would not allow it. Then the cost of war was deemed to be prohibitive; a nation resolving upon war faced bankruptcy and suicide. Even more we relied upon the peace propaganda with its hopeful appeal to prudence and imaginative pity, with its congresses and conferences and interparliamentary unions. Besides, had not Europe enjoyed a half-century of peace? But just as the world neighborhood was on the point of becoming a brotherhood, General von Emmich crossed the Belgian border—"the Rubicon which divides honor from infamy"—and the bells of destiny rang round the world. The trouble was that, apart from the fighting instinct inbred and consolidated by millenniums of battle, national boundaries were marked by electrified barbed wire. George shook hands with William over magazines of dynamite. Nicholas exchanged messages with Francis Joseph through a line of frowning fortresses. And now the nations fly at one another's throats with an energy and an equipment threatening the race itself along with the wealth of its achievements, the very intimacy of world relationships widening the range and enhancing the violence of the conflict.

We were at first surprised. A little later we were indignant and resentful that the European tragedy should stretch a red hand three thousand miles overseas to disturb our peace and reverse the policy of a hundred years. Later still we saw that hand clutching at the throat of America and dragging her in.

Then we saw our friends passing in khaki, and now at length we feel ourselves sucked into the maelstrom on its subtle and ghastly currents. With the exception of that moment in the midst of the ages from which all other times take their date, this is the greatest moment in history. Its four years' suffering and havoc exceed those of any previous century; its forces are twenty times as great as those of any other war; its issues—the moral law in state action, rule by inherited right or rule by the people, the possible recurrence of such a catastrophe—these issues are more fundamental and universal than any over which the iron dice of war ever before rattled. If they are decided adversely, the spiritual heritage of the race is forfeit and civilization disappears once again in the maw of barbarism.

Here is the gravest crisis which ever confronted the intelligence and character of the world. At such a time the routine of life is shattered, its veneering is stripped off bare to the elemental facts, hoary traditions are flouted, the intellectual and moral horizon lifts, contacts multiply, buried sins rise to condemn, wild dreams take body and draw near, nothing is radical, anything possible. At such a time we may slip into irremediable ruin, or spring dizzily to heights of social progress otherwise beyond our reach. Civilization's moulting time is come. Will she sicken and die, or deck herself in stronger, fairer forms for the delight and service of mankind?

As Ruskin pointed out years ago, war does call forth and use glorious human virtues, but war in itself is never glorious. I cannot fancy a book of doom big enough to record the guilt of the men who precipitated this atrocious war. But American participation for the defense of her national ideals and the ordered life of the world is as righteous as it is splendid. With President Wilson we are all proud to fight for mankind. The final issue cannot be doubtful. Meantime it throws a blood-red gauntlet at our feet, challenging our nation, our religion, our culture, and ourselves.

Let me speak briefly of the national challenge. On the oc-

casion of welcoming in Paris a section of the American Red
Cross, Bergson said that the French people in August, 1914,
felt that they were called to a formidable and superhuman
task, and they became grave and solemn as in a cathedral.
The men of France, said Kipling, have been wrought to an
edge of steel, and the women of France are a line of fire behind
them. So England has fused the classes, forgotten political
differences, healed industrial dissensions, and with unified and
tenacious resistance holds the fort till America comes for the
decisive blow. In a special sense does the challenge of the
Great War come to the United States: "Your democracy is
weak and inefficient. It lacks coördination and centralized
authority. Your composite assembly of different races, habits,
creeds, ideals, you will not be able to fuse into unity and co-
hesion, or harmonize to serve the national purpose. Your
people resent a strong government, and a few years will suffice
to break up your national life into warring factions." Such
is the challenge. Again, America was the first to establish
government of the people, for the people, and by the people.
Will it save that principle in the final struggle with autocracy?
Will it justify representative government now? Let three issues
of Liberty Bonds oversubscribed answer. Let a twenty-billion-
dollar annual budget answer. Let a million and a half boys
in khaki answer.

There is another challenge. A brilliant Irishman shortly
before his tragic death in France wrote: "When this great
war fell on Europe those who knew even a little of current
ethical and political ideas felt that Europe had once more been
threatened by barbarism; Odin had thrown down his last
challenge to Christ." The challenge is very real and very
sharp. Let me specify.

It involves, in the first place, the moral order. The insane
philosopher whose most important book will be found in every
German soldier's kit, and who is most influential among German intellectuals, declares flatly: "All history is the experi-

mental refutation of the theory of the so-called moral order of things." The moral law is flouted with apparent impunity. Has it been abrogated? Perhaps its author has lost interest or is dead. May I not defy the universe and survive? Right is what an intelligent man wants to do and can do; wrong what he wants to do and cannot do! And religion—what is that but a refined superstition?

Your hearts have already made answer. The stars in their courses fight against sin. Character does count. And the Government of the United States recognizes and proceeds upon that understanding. "If you would shoot straight, you must live straight," said the Secretary of the Navy to his blue-jackets. The Secretary of War has declared that the Commission of Training Camp Activities, of which the Young Men's Christian Association is so conspicuous a feature, is one of the most important factors in winning the war. And who of you doubts that the heroism and fortitude which have made the name of France doubly dear in these last days are compounded of her native gifts of "dreaming, generosity, and the soaring spirit" fused by the flame of devotion to home and God? A young lieutenant wrote home, "I am not a Christian and a soldier; I am a Christian soldier."

Faith in Providence is challenged by the blood and darkness of the time. It is freely said that human life is emptied of its purpose. History has lost consistency. The reins have been dropped, and the fiery steeds of human destiny fly crashing into utter wreck. The intellectual horizon, which is the best fruit of your culture, supplies the refutation. It discovers the race fighting its way up from the jungle and come at length to its present stage, as if led by an Unseen Hand from one battleground of darkness to another, always toward the day. It shows us still fighting and blundering, indeed, but it shows also a pitying Providence still hedging our steps to a wide place of peace in righteousness. Your view into the far past justifies the assurance that this same Providence will ultimately eman-

cipate us from our brute inheritance, settle in the constitution
of all sections of the race the moral standards which now control the highest, and establish the nations in universal brotherhood wherein the good of each will be the care of all. "Watchman, what of the night?" "The morning cometh!"

Let me say, further, that the bloody gauntlet of the World
War lies at the door of the Church, challenging at once its
efficacy as a force in human affairs and the validity of its message. As they watched bags of treasure carried in through
the gates of the Lateran Church at Rome, Pope Innocent IV
said to Saint Thomas Aquinas: "The day is past when the
Church could say, 'Silver and gold have I none'." Saint
Thomas replied: "Yes, Holy Father, and the day is past
when the Church could say to the lame man, 'Rise up and
walk'." The Church has wealth; has it power? Does it meet
the needs of men on the levels of daily human life? Does it
bear burdens, console and inspire, or split hairs 'twixt south
and southwest side? Does it speak the authoritative word of
rebuke of wrong in high places, of guidance in perplexity, of
assurance and hope? That clear-souled, radiant Christian,
Donald Hankey, writing out of intimate association with the
British soldier in the trenches of France, and presenting his
practical conception of the aloofness of the Church, says the
present crisis is an unprecedented opportunity for the Church
of England either to make a new start or to commit suicide.

What answer does your Christian culture make to such a
challenge? It will not do to ignore it as foreign to your relatively sheltered and untossed experience. It is pressing in
now upon every type of experience, even the most remote and
unresponsive. You must take up this challenge also. You
will help forward the movement already well advanced which
is shifting the emphasis of Christian interest from opinion to
conduct, from metaphysics to unselfish service. You will insist upon coöperation in the divided body of Christ, and upon

an ampler adjustment to the moving world which it is set to transform. At the same time, you will assert that the Church as the instrument of religion is regnant in human life. It is the agency of the coming Kingdom of God to pluck up the root of moral evil out of which all social wrong springs. There can be no new and better world following this crisis, no reconstructed social order after the mind of Christ, apart from the reconstruction of the units of society. It is not a new social mechanism that we want, but a new social spirit. Not new laws, but new people. And it is the primary function of the Christian Church to make of men and women new creatures in Christ Jesus. As another has pointed out, the three historic scourges of mankind—famine, pestilence, war—have counted their victims by the tens of millions. The first two have been mastered—famine by commerce, pestilence by science. But war, instead of yielding to pestilence or science, is in reality born in commerce and trained to superhuman destructiveness by science. "Only religion can kill war, for religion alone creates the new heart."

Education cannot hope to escape the transforming influence of this critical time. It is likely to be molded in all its stages into more vital relation to the actual interests and activities of men and women. But a more radical demand is widely made. Our problems are practical problems, it is said; why should not education equip us to solve them? What we require is practical efficiency. Let education produce it, or give over its claims. This breadth of human sympathy, this intellectual horizon which has grown up in you by years of study of the best which has been thought and said in the world, is challenged by the German ideal of economic efficiency reflected in not a little of the current insistence upon vocational training. The masters of thought and song and story of the far past—what did they know of the apparatus of our modern life, of our labor and transportation problems, of our social needs and aspirations? Why lose precious time with them? And these inspirers of the inner life of man—they butter no parsnips in the hungry, struggling world today!

Permit me to remind you that man is body and soul. What shall it profit a man if he gain the whole world and lose his soul, and what shall a man give in exchange for his soul? Germany has lost her soul to gain the world. Belgium has lost the world to gain her soul. Of course, the economic foundations of life must be secure, but we are not called on to surrender our spiritual heritage. The esthetic and spiritual elements of our life are as real as the physical, and the culture which ignores them is as degrading as it is partial.

For you, gentlemen, the keenest challenge of this fateful hour is the personal challenge. An eighteen-year-old French soldier, in the grave moment before a bayonet charge, wrote : "When war is over and I go home, I must be a changed being. I shall have no right to be as I formerly was. Through the war mankind must be reborn, and it is our duty to be reborn first of all." As I signed today the diplomas of the Class of 1918, almost every other one bore the name of a comrade now somewhere in the line of bloody steel from the Channel to the Swiss Border, or getting ready to go. And many of you who hear me now will shortly take your life in your hand and join the crusade for human rights. That baptism of fire will certainly consume you or cleanse you. That blood-spattered experience will not leave you the same. Like the French lad, you will be "reborn." For the seeds of generosity and self-sacrifice, of consecration to the high and noble things of life, must yield a harvest of new life on a loftier plane for yourselves first of all and then for the coming regenerate society of which you are the heralds and champions.

And those of you who are not called to this special service are anointed with the same chrism. With a like consecration you will labor at the foundations of a new social order, while your brothers defend it. We shall need clean hearts and clear heads for after-war reconstruction and adjustment. Intellectual leadership and the Christian motive find their opportunity in such a time. Be true, my brothers; be true! Make sure your harmony with the Divine will. Refresh yourselves in weariness or perplexity by the assurance of the Divine support. And whether you "dice with death while the mad guns curse overhead," or in more homely ways give yourselves wholly to the highest you see and the best you know, live or die, not for flag, or clan, or class,

> But for a dream born in an artisan's shed
> And for the secret Scripture of the poor.

CULTURE AND THE UNFINISHED WAR

1919

In the Dream of Fair Women, Tennyson sings of "the spacious times of great Elizabeth." Early in the reign of that remarkable queen there was a notable quickening of the national life in England and of the general intelligence. The increase of wealth provided a larger leisure and raised the standard of culture and refinement. The England of the period, moreover, participated in the more general influence of the restlessness and curiosity of the age. The new heavens of Copernicus, Kepler, and Galileo, and the new earth of Columbus and Drake, widened enormously the intellectual horizon. The races of men discovered one another in the prevailing passion for foreign travel. Nothing was wanting for the opening of a new epoch in English achievement but the signal. That signal was given in the national triumph over Spain with the destruction of the Catholic menace, and a new England glorified by a new and unmatched literature sprang forward into the leadership of the world.

And these times in which your careers will be made are likewise spacious times, with a horizon quite without precedent in all history. In the realm of science, there has been, indeed, no discovery of first-rate dignity, though the recognition of the X-rays, the Hertzian waves, and the complex structure of the atom are of very great practical and theoretical importance. But the push and promise, the liberalizing effect, of the evolution conception of the last century are still potent in the larger life of our period. The applications of science have lately put all natural elements into service to man. Our knowledge of the earth extends from pole to pole on the surface, and from six miles above the surface to its flaming center below. Economic and political relations are established with all sections of the human race. And in upon these quiet processes of expansion there burst in 1914, with hardly a premonitory tremor, the eruption of the World War. Its devastation is now ended, the fiery flood subsided, and we look out upon a new world deeply chastened and suffering, but repentant and greatly purified, open and responsive to a new leadership.

As for ourselves, the German menace outraged us and wrought us to the highest pitch of unity, consecration, and sacrifice. That menace was blocked and obliterated when our national endeavor was but barely launched, and we now turn to look into one another's faces with dilated eyes wonderingly, hardly yet seeing the import and far reaches of the magnificent achievement. Still under the spell of the enterprise which at once elated and melted us, we stand here today with a feeling of emancipation and new-found capacities, in full view of horizons of opportunity and duty absolutely unparalleled, imperial in scope and imperious like the call of destiny.

Many of you wanted to go to France—were actually in training when the armistice was signed. Well, the war is not over. For consider its aims and see whether they are achieved and secure. There could be no clearer, no nobler expression of those aims than that of April 2, 1917, by the man who led "this great and peaceful people into the most terrible and disastrous of all wars." "We shall fight," said he, "for the things which we have always carried nearest our hearts—for democracy, for the right of those who submit to authority to have a voice in their own government, for the rights and liberties of small nations, for the universal dominion of right by such a concert of free peoples as will bring peace and safety to all nations, and make the world itself at last free." In the Mount Vernon address on Independence Day, the following year, he condensed the great objects for which the associated peoples were fighting into these weighty words: "What we seek is the reign of law, based upon the consent of the governed and sustained by the organized opinion of mankind."

What has been done so far is the taking of certain important outposts of these great objectives, clearing the ground, equipping the forces, planning the campaign for winning them all ultimately.   For example, we have discovered that, even in the chemic and mechanical warfare of our time, the decisive factor is still the man behind the shell and the bayonet.   To maintain this unit of victory in maximum efficiency is, accordingly, the first consideration, and the War Department demonstrated its wisdom and its modernness nowhere more clearly than in its discipline of physical and moral sanitation.   Beyond question, what is good in war time for the efficiency of the soldier is good in peace time for the efficiency of the citizen.   This war policy does not end with the war.   Eight days before the armistice, Secretary Baker said, "I do not know when this war against the German Empire will come to an end, but I know this, that the war for the salvation of young American manhood has only just begun, and it is going to keep on."

And how stands our aim of universal peace?   Is the late war the last war?   I remind you that some men among us, assuming to stand on the rock of scientific fact, laugh to scorn the idealism which hopes to change by pious resolutions at a peace table the fighting instinct of man consolidated by millenniums of battle ; and they are insisting upon universal military training and other preparation for the next war.   There are others shamelessly attacking the Covenant of the League of Nations, the first great effort to organize the opinion of mankind in support of righteousness and justice and against the folly and the crime of war.   Some of these critics honestly doubt that such a covenant will be able to restrain any signatory which may choose to consider it but another "scrap of paper."   Other critics are still citizens of the isolated republic of Washington's day, and, misinterpreting the Farewell Address, decline to recognize our unavoidable and established international relationships and responsibilities.   But the most shocking and disheartening group of League critics, under cover of a perfervid nationalism, are playing politics with that great instrument, and, in this hour of suffering and promised renovation, threaten the world with the return to the tinkering and trading of back-stairs diplomacy, through which the dimmest eyes can see looming the red terror of a blind and passionate anarchy. They want no coöperation with the enlightened nations of the world to secure the common good; it would compromise the national advantage in world trade for which they scheme. They want no self-determination for anybody except ourselves; we may want Mexico some day. They want no reduction of armaments; it would restrict big business, whose bursting coffers supply the best political capital. And so you see that the crushing of militarism on the fields of France, while of the highest importance, is no guarantee against its rising again in Europe—in this free republic of the west. The war to end war and to establish the supremacy of the moral law in State action is not yet won. What we have won is the preliminary campaign, not the war.

You will probably agree that the same is true of another great American aim and justification in the war, namely, democracy. The essence of democracy is twofold, involving both a view and a spirit. The view is that man as man is of inherent worth without regard to position or possessions, and that he has, therefore, the right of self-development and self-determination within the boundaries of the social fellowship to which he belongs; outside it he may not go either to desert or to attack it. The spirit of democracy is the spirit of justice, brotherhood, and coöperation, as against class-consciousness and prejudice, as against special privilege and an artificial and irresponsible control. This view and spirit combine in the democratic attitude.

What, now, has been the effect of the war upon this great conception? We have witnessed the bankruptcy of force as the principle of national action and the defeat of irresponsible control. Germany, which was the standing menace to the happiness and freedom of the average man, is humiliated and broken, and the ex-Kaiser, the embodiment of an artificial and arrogant overlordship, is trembling today in exile. At least the forms of a government responsible to the people have been established in the room of the old autocracy. We have won the first campaign in the war for democracy. We have not yet won the war for democracy. That war is not yet over. Democracy is not yet established and secure in the political, industrial, and social life of the world. Are we able to say that it is established and secure in the life of our own country? I do not refer, of course, to equality of endowment, or position, or private fortune. Men are not born equal, and their station and property are not equal, because they both are achieved. I refer, rather, to equality of privilege and opportunity. Does not the average man still wait for assurance of tomorrow's bread and of regular employment? Has our democracy yet provided against the contingencies of old age? Does not the average man yet wait for his emancipation from the hard conditions under which he lives and works?—from the manipulation of men who make gain of his weakness?—from the ignorance which makes democracy a peril? Have many of our American democracies done much more than trifle with the education of the average citizen, of whom they expect in theory an intelligent self-determination and citizenship? The task of democratizing industry is yet before us—giving the workers representation in the direction of enterprises and a fair share in the profits which they produce, shifting the industrial system from the basis of competition to the basis of coöperation, from the basis of making private profits to the basis of rendering public service.

It appears, accordingly, that none of the primary aims of the United States and her associates in the European War—permanent world peace, control of state action by moral law, democracy—has been fully realized. What then? Simply this: we are called to press the war through to final victory.

If blood and treasure were not idly spent for these great causes, if our millions of boys in khaki went really, as we said, on a holy crusade, and if not in vain thousands of them "poured out the red sweet wine of youth" to bring in the better day, we have no other life task but to complete theirs, and that in the same spirit of gallantry and consecration. One who mingled with them tells us that they knew that God was awaiting them just beyond the next moment, or that they had a rendezvous with Him the day following or that day fortnight; they were engaged in His business and expected to report to Him soon.

You certainly will not break faith with your brothers who lie under the poppies of Flanders. You put off khaki in December. Today you still wear the uniform of the Christian soldier, and it has just now been adorned with the insignia of Christian culture. In this significant moment of your personal experience, in this critical moment of the development of civilization, seal anew your vows of allegiance to the Kingdom of God, in which are comprehended all the fundamental issues of the unfinished war. Establish once for all your connection with unfailing supplies of the Christian impulse, and steady your will to victory by a fresh surrender, daily repeated, of your capacity and your equipment to Christ, the conquering Friend of Man. Make Him the idol of your heart and the Master of your thinking. Give Him here now any part of your personality which He does not already possess. Make Him King of your will and Lord of your life. But do not forget that He is more than that. He is King of kings and Lord of lords. He saves a man; that is His pledge that He will save man. His reign in the individual life is the guarantee of His reign in the social life. I am not quite sure that I want Him to save me if He will not save my brothers of the world. Doubt anything except Him. Doubt, if you must, any item of current theological statements; for who made these statements but certain gentlemen of this or the former time, more or less qualified to make them? Doubt any item of the creeds, but never doubt Him. For the deepest infidelity is the fear that His dream of the Divine Will realized in human life is only a dream, beautiful, indeed, but insubstantial and illusory—the fear that He will see of the travail of His soul and be dissatisfied. No, no! By the burdens He has lifted, by the fetters He has broken, by the doors He has opened, by the rising levels of life wherever He has walked among men, by the hopes He raised in His dark time brightening through the centuries to this august hour, His dream is coming true. I see even now some of the kings and the nations, and, a little way down the vista of coming years, the last of them, bringing their glory and honor unto Him, and I seem to hear faintly what must be the great voices in Heaven, saying, "The kingdoms of this world are become the Kingdoms of our Lord and of His Christ; and He shall reign forever and ever."

CULTURE AND PROGRESS

1920

You are eager and ready to go, ready in the settled purpose of serving the need of the world, in having determined the form of service you will undertake, in the equipment of self-mastery and developed and trained powers. But I hold you yet a moment in leash to renew our pledges of loyalty to one another and to the great causes which have won our hearts, to visualize the social situation in which you will find your place and task, and to assure you this last time before we separate of the one way out of it, the only law and method of social progress.

In the fundamentals of human life, its essential activities and needs, the modern world is like the ancient. Perhaps the sharpest contrast appears at the point where science gave man control of his environment and precipitated the industrial revolution of the eighteenth and nineteenth centuries. "In the drab surroundings of the workshop, in the silent mystery of the laboratory, began the magic of the new age." Its symbols are steam and electricity. More recently the World War has added a deeper tone to this contrast, extending it inward from the modes of life to moral and intellectual attitudes. We now recognize two phenomena which, in their practical universality, we are justified in calling new. I refer to democracy and internationalism. The world is now nine tenths democratic, and the United States Senate and Mexico together present a negligible remainder of a bumptious and exclusive nationalism. All the rest of the world is organized on the basis of international justice and goodwill.

In this new world we are come upon a critical and decisive hour. The situation is electric with anxiety and hope. Society appears a maze of injustice and inequality. A clinging fog magnifies what it does not wholly hide. Over the eastern horizon we descry the wild eyes and shaggy whiskers of social

[106]

revolution. The blind Sampson of labor seems to be feeling for the pillars which support the social order. The equilibrium of production and consumption is everywhere unsettled. By the applications of science the power of each man to produce goods has been increased fifty-fold, and yet for multitudes of men the most elementary wants remain unsatisfied, and the conditions under which the poor fight the endless battle for bread continue as hard as ever they were. In continental Europe the destruction which wasted at noonday is followed by the pestilence that walketh in darkness, and we are now authoritatively informed that it will require $500,-000,000 to save from starvation the next few months masses of people stretching from the Baltic to the Black Sea. Habitual restraints are grown lax. The fighting spirit which we built up in all our able-bodied young men refuses to be exorcised overnight on the signing of the armistice. The severity of military discipline is succeeded by the infection of moral license, and an unprecedented crime wave is on all over the world.

But the situation, if critical, is not hopeless. The bottom has not dropped out; it is only leaky. Things are not gone to the eternal bow-wows; they only seem headed that way. We must not give way to panic. There are considerations on the other side. The problem of industrial unrest, for example, is the same sort of problem as that with which we have long been familiar in the individual case of the discontented business man, the indifferent student, the theological heretic, the egotist whose abilities do not justify his ambitions, and, while such maladjustments of personal instincts to a repressing environment are troublesome, they must not be allowed unduly to alarm us. Remember, further, that in this very period the social passion has mounted in temperature to a point never reached before. There is such a fact as the public conscience, and the movement toward coöperation in all spheres of life is pronounced and growing. Those lofty steel tentacles at Arlington feeling in the empty air for the movements of the human spirit in far distant climes are a token of the interdependence and comity of man. As a distinguished American has said, "God has made us neighbors; now let justice make us friends."

The problems of human life are all reducible to two—the problem of living and the problem of living together. Inasmuch as every individual life is bound up with every other, these two problems are at bottom one—the problem of living together. Christian and non-Christian, native and alien, white and black, intelligent and ignorant, vigorous and feeble, old and young, generous and grasping, male and female, every one of us absolutely unique, the first and last of a kind—living together in the family, the neighborhood, the state, and the world. Some among us insist that after twenty centuries of Christian history we cannot live together except under the law of the jungle. Might is right. Let the strong rule the weak. It hath been so, it is so now, and shall be so to the end. The ultimate test of strength is war—war of individuals; war of the classes, labor with its votes, capital with its money, the farmer with his products, the manufacturer and tradesman with their prices; war of the nations—*Deutschland über Alles!* America against the world! This is Prussianism whether it speaks in Berlin or in Washington!

Other students of society take the opposite position. They remember the words of the Master of Men and Times: "One is your teacher and all you are brothers." Men are not apes and tigers, though there are apes and tigers among them. You know the old legend that at times men become wolves and get into their old skins again. There are, indeed, in civilized countries millions of men whose mental and moral equipment places them on a plane with barbarians and savages. It is a long road and a bloody one by which we have traveled from the jungle to New York and Paris, with, I am afraid, not a little plunder of the jungle in our baggage and not a little law of the jungle in our ways. But the jungle is many millenniums behind us. The masses of men know it. Only the heredi-

tary ruling class ignores it and reenacts the battle of the jungle
to solidify and extend its power, or in democratic states in-
vestors and market seekers in foreign lands capitalize a perfervid nationalism, egging it on to war for purely economic
ends. If we must live together at all, we must live together
as brothers. This is Christianity.

Society has suffered many things of many physicians and is
little bettered. Indeed, the Prussian treatment, the latest applied, well-nigh wrecked it. After the culmination and utter
collapse of the anti-Christian method, are we not ready to look
frankly about us for another way out? Certainly now, if never
before, we have need of the sober and open mind, clear vision,
and an aggressive and heroic consecration. Is it the law of social progress that we seek—of progress from bad to good, from
good to better, from better to best unwaveringly? Then we
stand at the parting of the ways. The issue goes to the roots
of things. If we fall into error, we shall but revive the old antagonism of the classes, renew the old oscillation between progress and barbarism, and struggle painfully up out of the stupid
havoc of one war into preparation for another. If we find the
truth and give ourselves whole-heartedly to it, we shall become
knights of the new order riding forth to redress human wrongs,
to correct human abuses, to relieve human sufferings, to forestall the folly and crime of war, to be a living breakwater
against the flood of personal and national selfishness which
threatens all the higher interests of mankind with destruction,
to build the new humanity.

I make no apology for seeking the true law of social progress
in the thought of Jesus. He was the greatest social revolution-
ist in history. His aim was the loftiest, His consecration to it
the most absolute, His method the most radical, and, in spite
of the misreading, shortcomings and defection of His representatives, His actual achievement is the most far-reaching
and permanent. Wherever He appears He speaks the word
of emancipation. He launched the largest and most beneficent

movement in history. The most important items in the inventory of social progress are His gifts to mankind. The practical results which have followed His teachings everywhere attest His penetration, His wisdom, and His authority in the leadership of the race. He said, "I am the way."

What, then, is the secret and method of Jesus? It is certainly not the method of the Socialists who quote Him. For they ignore the root of moral evil out of which all social mischief grows. They blunder again in supposing that social relations are formal, mechanical, and consequently that the social scheme may be shaken to pieces today and put to rights tomorrow by act of Congress. On the contrary, social relations are personal relations and therefore moral relations. Accordingly, we shall never get on from industrial competition to coöperation by the Socialist highway, nor settle any of our problems by the Socialist method. It is not new legislation, or a new mechanism of government, or a new social scheme that we require. It is new people. Civilization, says an English cynic, is the disease produced by the effort to build a just society out of rotten material.

The method of Jesus, in Matthew Arnold's phrasing, is the method of inwardness; His secret, the secret of renunciation. He wrote no ideal commonwealth. He left no specifications for the construction of the ideal society. This fact has been misinterpreted as indicating want of interest in the organized life of man. What He did was to set up a new standard. He inspired a new life and trusted it to take its fit embodiment and expression. "All that He required of men wherewith to save them was a cross whereon to die." His redemption of the social unit guarantees the redemption of society. He would achieve social righteousness by the leaven of individual righteousness. According to Him, there can be no sure progress, no permanent social reconstruction in justice and good will, apart from individual renewal and the acceptance by us all of the law of the Cross as the law of life. If now, as Bernard Shaw suggests, we give Christianity a trial in our program of social progress, this is what is involved. It will do nothing unless it does this deepest thing—transform the individual life, infect it with the ideal of the Kingdom of Heaven, and train it for the work of the Kingdom. To this program of Christ and this law of Christ your experience, training, and ideals irrevocably commit you.

And now, my brothers, I give you the leash, I release you to your careers. It is a great day for great souls—let little ones take care!—boundless horizons, gulfs to wash you down. On the stormy coast of northwest France the Breton mariner, when he puts out to sea, prays: "My God, protect me, my ship is so little, Thy ocean so great." God speed you! God protect you and bring every little ship to port at length!

CULTURE AND INTERNATIONALISM

1921

Your college career coincides with perhaps the most eventful period of our national history. You entered here just five months after the declaration of war with Germany. You mobilized your intellectual and financial resources for the college campaign while the country was mobilizing its resources of men, enterprises, and institutions for the European campaign. You participated in the emotional response of the time, deep, universal, culminating in that subtle and irresistible combination of enthusiasm and anger called morale. In our mental life also there was an enormous quickening and expansion. But the outstanding feature of our national life was its overflow into new channels. Our pent-up nationalism broke over into internationalism, and for some tragic and noble months we were citizens of the world and champions of the rights of man. Materialists and politicians of the opposition maintain that we went to Europe solely to save the United States, and that it is delusive and mischievous to attribute primarily to "a tender susceptibility" the American proffer of the helping hand. But you and I know that it was the voice of our great President that stirred the soul of our people. "That grave voice," as a distinguished Britisher said, "sounding majestically above the shrill rhetoric of European statesmen, carried with it the promise of a new world, and for the first time in history there stepped into the arena a nation that had no ends of her own to gain, and stood for Right, for Humanity, and for nothing else." There was no chaffering and bargaining about what we should get in return for the national sacrifice. We were quite content to give the rein to our generous impulses. If they swept us into complications from which it might be difficult to withdraw, that would be seen to in its time. Let the boys ride far ; we should hope for most of them back. Let the treasure flow free and exhaustingly; maybe it could be replenished in after years, maybe not. We could not stop to figure. The trumpets blew down all the winds of the world, and we must be off! At a bound our smug aloofness was behind us.

As I have thought of your leave-taking today on the victorious completion of your college campaign, of the ripening of your culture in these heroic and expansive years, and of the close-knit world of men where lie your tasks, it has been impossible to suppress or evade the one theme which emerges from the situation. I must have a few words with you on *Culture and Internationalism.*

What is internationalism? The word was first used with reference to international law. It came later to mean the principle of forcing a weak country to submit to the control of several stronger nations. Its present meaning is different from either of these. It may now be defined as the cosmopolitan sense of human relations, the recognition by one nation of the rights of all nations, the coöperation of independent nations to secure their integrity and promote their common interests. Such a fellowship of nations was, of course, impossible before the rise of modern sovereign states in the sixteenth century. The break-up of the Roman Empire resulted in a social situation not unlike that of primitive man. Small groups gathered about strong men in loose contact, without roads or law or administration. Certain of these loosely coherent groups grew gradually into kingdoms, of which the first to emerge from the wreckage was the kingdom of the Franks. France and Germany came out of it. They were united until 840, when they drew apart and began the long tragedy which culminated in 1914.

Internationalism, as we now know it, was likewise impossible before the development of the gigantic machinery of communications which has gone far toward unifying the modern world. Rejecting the possibility of the union of Great Britain and the American colonies, Edmund Burke explained that nature in-

8

tervened—"I cannot remove the eternal barriers of the creation." But the "eternal barrier" of the Atlantic has been removed by the steamship and the airplane, and Smuts and Wilson from the ends of the earth meet Orlando and Lloyd George in conference at Paris after a few days of luxurious travel. And the winged Mercury, electricity, puts national representatives at the international council table in immediate communication with their home governments.

International law from its beginning with Grotius applied moral standards to state action, and an increasing number of treaties set practical limits to the doctrine of national absolutism. International conferences to promote the common wellbeing belong also in this development, whose pre-war culmination was the Hague Peace Conferences. And yet these Conferences recognized the absolute sovereignty of states, their right to make war, only prescribing the method of conducting it, and had no word about the obligations or political relations of states. It was left for the World War to draw this issue sharply and on a planetary scale. Germany was the embodiment and champion of exclusive nationalism and absolute sovereignty. The Allies, at first merely resisting the menace of vassalage and destruction, came later, under Wilson's inspiration and leadership, to be the embodiment and champions of the supremacy of the moral law, of the rights of man, of the integrity and self-determination of the weaker nations. These aims came to be synonymous with civilization, and the struggle was a struggle between civilization and barbarism. The oscillating line of the Western Front marked the recession and advance of civilization. There internationalism was born, became a cause, a passion, almost a religion. It led straight to the League of Nations. That covenant was the greatest and most promising of human documents for the coöperation of all men against the stupidity and crime of war and for the promotion of the law of justice and fraternity among nations. American rejection of it was as disastrous as it was irrational, a

reversal of the dearly bought moral progress of the race.   We
lapsed shamefully from the high mood of 1917 and '18 into
the absolutism and selfish isolation which we had fought to
destroy.   Our position is indefensible from any angle.

How is internationalism related to nationalism?   There is
no necessary opposition between them.   Everybody except the
politician knows that internationalism presupposes independent
nationalities and does not compromise national integrity, but
guarantees it.   Nationalism, or patriotism, is an instinctive
group loyalty.   Your own romantic attachment to Alma Mater
is an example on a lesser scale.   It is a non-rational sense of
community, a sort of extended self, determining partiality to
one's own group.   "Good or bad," we say, "it is mine—my
family, my clan, my college, my state, my country, right or
wrong."   It does not assert itself until it is challenged.   College spirit requires an intercollegiate contest to call it out, and
so patriotism is hardly conscious in times of peace.   The instinct of self-preservation in the individual becomes on the national scale state sovereignty whose only law is the national
advantage, whose sole obligation is to its own citizens.   Machiavelli wrote the philosophy of this absolute sovereignty and
selfishness, and diplomats are its high priests.   Voltaire's dictum might serve as their motto—"Take no interest in anything
that goes on beyond the limits of your own cabbage garden."
Their independence of the moral law is illustrated in the con-
fession of one of the greatest of them.   "If we had done for
ourselves," said Cavour, "what we have done for Italy, we
should have been great rascals."

Let me ask now what is the relation of culture to this great
new idea of internationalism?   Just a year ago there met in
Brussels the international Union of Academies.   It is a scientific federation of learned societies in America, Belgium, Den-
mark, France, Great Britain, Greece, Holland, Poland, Italy,
Russia, and Japan, to secure coöperation in the advancement
of studies.   A year ago the International Federation of Uni-

versity Women met in London with representatives from fifteen countries. A Pan-Pacific educational Congress is called for Honolulu next August. Examples of world-wide association to promote common intellectual interests might be multiplied indefinitely. A philosopher of Germany writes lectures in English and delivers them in Scotland, and declares that his book is witness that culture, moral, intellectual, and esthetic, is not limited by the bounds of nationality. That in 1908. Years before that date a famous French critic said, "While we are good Frenchmen we yet admit the superiority of the Germans and the English in many ways." Scholarship is essentially international. Culture is cosmopolitan, human, public. It has many marks, as a certain gentility and refinement of manner, moderation, inward wealth, and intellectual satisfactions. Its chief mark, however, is range of interests, a tolerance and a breadth of sympathy, in a word, horizon. But the culture which grows up in the atmosphere of positive Christianity adds to horizon fellowship, sees in aliens brothers, and knows no boundaries racial or political in the universality of its service. It is not surprising, therefore, that college men have what Mr. Wells calls the international mind. If a debate on the question of internationalism is announced between a United States senator and a Harvard president you know beforehand their choice of sides.

My last inquiry concerns itself with the obligations of a man of culture in the present situation, his attitude and his opportunity. To be more direct, what may we reasonably expect of you in this era of internationalism? For I warn you against supposing the American contradiction to be anything more than exceptional and temporary. There are already signs of a popular revulsion at the shameful isolation into which partisan politics forced our great country. In response to that rising sentiment the government is taking carefully guarded steps toward reëntering the maze of European public problems. Very truly, gentlemen, you stand in the morning of a new day,

and thereon I do felicitate you.   To the inspiration of its early
dews and growing brightness I know you will respond.   You
will retain your primary allegiance to your own mother, but
respect the mothers of other men.   If the United States, when
once the war was won, fell back selfishly into the narrow nation-
alistic horizon, you will help her up to the larger human view.

Certainly our late experience has shown that local interests
are bound up in one bundle with those of all other nations.
The problems of this world relationship will not be solved by
governments and diplomats, whom we have to thank for our
present troubles.   The aristocratic sections of society stand for
the old diplomacy of national pride and selfishness.   The problems of racial and national contacts must be settled at last by
the people, by men and women of good will controlled by the
Christian spirit of fraternity and justice informed and guided
by men of vision.   For example, is war inevitable?   Yes, until
the policies of sovereign states are changed.   But what are
states and state policies?   A state is a settled group of men and
women living under a government which they approve.   And
the policy of a state is the way the men and women who speak
for the group have decided to treat the men and women of
another group.   We shall be caught in a net of sophistries and
get nowhere, if we speak of the state and nation as abstractions,
as things apart from the people who constitute them.   To
change the national policy, you have to change the people.

And here springs up squarely in front of you your chief duty
as trained citizens of a great republic with widening and commanding relations to the rest of the world.   It calls you to
create and guide a public opinion which cannot be "duped by
misrepresentation nor misled by passion," to realize, within
the sphere of your influence, the world hope of the time—
when all men's good shall

> Be each man's rule, and universal Peace
> Lie like a shaft of light across the land
> And like a lane of beams athwart the sea
> Through all the circle of the golden year.

CULTURE AND CONSECRATION

1922

The greatest of German poets said of the greatest of French emperors, in a time which set all capacities in motion, that he had so distinguished himself as to become, in spite of his obscure origin, the idol of a nation of thirty millions when he was only twenty-seven years of age. "Yes, yes," continued Goethe, "one must be young to do great things. If I were prince, I should have young men in the highest offices; but they must have capacities and be endowed with clearness and energy and also with the best and noblest character." It is just as true today as it was in the time of Napoleon that the world belongs to youth. For youth maintains the worth and the joy of life against the complaint and disillusionment of age. The splendid courage of youth is undaunted before any problem or task. It has not been disciplined by the experience of defeat. Indeed, the distinguishing traits of youth—its openness to new ideas, its gift of enthusiasm, its boundless energy, its spirit of adventure—are the very conditions of achievement, and, when inspired and knitted together by a noble purpose, are the essential factors of heroism.

You see, gentlemen, my first thought about you today is that you are young. In your presence I feel the glow and thrill of my own long-past youth—its vow to be clear and true, its wide-ranging passion to know, its untutored ambition to set a high standard of public service. And you are dreaming and pledging. The atmosphere which envelops us is soft and bright and holy. It pulses with tenderness and solicitude, with promise and daring. It is aglow with the spirit of adventure and consecration. In such a moment, so freighted with memories, so tender with the whispers of happy loves, so radiant with the sense of release, so tremblingly expectant on the margin of your career, permit me to lead you to the altar and take the vows of your young manhood and pledge your Christian culture to its proper tasks in the blind and blundering world into which you now pass.

For culture, however satisfying and charming it may be, is not an end in itself. The first motive which ought to impel us to study may be, as Montesquieu said, to augment the excellence of our nature and to make an intelligent being yet more intelligent, but that is not the last motive. An enriched and trained intelligence, a moral sense enlightened and disciplined, refinement of manners, tastes and feelings, generosity and tolerance of spirit, are the badges of culture wherever they appear, and they adorn any life. Culture, however, is not ornament, but equipment. A barren intellectualism is without justification.

> Know, not for knowing's sake,
> But to become a star to men forever.

And when the Christian ideal and aim are added to this culture, it is driven out into the highways of human intercourse to spend itself in serving human needs.

> Knowledge thou has lent,
> But, Lord, the will—there lies the bitter need ;
> Give us to build about the deep intent
>   The deed, the deed.
> Grant us the will to fashion as we feel,
>   Grant us the strength to labor as we know,
> Grant us the purpose, ribbed and edged with steel,
>   To strike the blow.

I pledge you first of all to be true to your civic duties. Whatever your career may be, you cannot escape the responsibilities of citizenship. As a private citizen you will support the society of which you are a member and whose benefits you enjoy. It would be dishonorable to accept the advantages of ordered society and to decline its obligations. Among the most dangerous enemies of the social order are sometimes found men who like you have had the best training under Christian

ideals.   In some cases they are preoccupied, in others superior.
The political life in all its levels is to them an offensive scramble.
And so they leave the administration of the public business
and the selection of public servants to the ignorant or to the
cunning and energy of the organized enemies of society.   Many
of you will be called to public duty in the State and Nation.
Answer the call.   The relative inferiority of American public
officials in intellectual background and horizon, as well as in
equipment for the positions which they occupy, is due, in part,
to the fact that we regard politics as a profession, rather than
a service ; in part, to the fact that fit men so often stand aloof ;
and, in part, to the irrelevant considerations which control
appointment to office.   What a spectacle does any session of
Congress or General Assembly present of self-seeking, partisan-
ship, delays, bartering, buncombe, and all-round incompetence.   I do not say there are no men of intelligence and character in the public service.   There are many.   I am charging
you to increase the number.

In the social life of this troubled but hopeful time, you are
called to be practical idealists : men who are controlled by
the great ideals of democracy, justice, and fraternity, and who
stand for the application of Christian principles to the settlement of personal, national, and international problems ; but
men who see no short cut to the millennium, who recognize
the actual conditions under which progress must be made.   Do
not surrender the ideals of internationalism and the peace of
the world, social justice, industrial democracy, equality of opportunity, supremacy of law.   But do not compromise the
ideal by ignoring the obstacles in the way of realizing it.   Deny
the economic interpretation of life, but do not deny its economic
foundations.   Consider the circumstances, but not unduly.
That way lie hesitation and defeat.   Keep your eye on the
ideal, the noble sentiment, the just action, and strike the proper
and adequate blow for it.   Make it hard for the circumstances.
Consult "brass-tacks" philosophers ; reject their philosophy.

I pledge your culture to the culture of others.   Education is the chief business of any community, rural or urban.   Agriculture is subordinate to child culture.   Indeed, agriculture is justified by the contribution it can be made to make to the happiness and security of the future by providing adequately for the children of the present.   The wheels of industry turn for the same high purpose, or they would best not turn at all. The rewards of trade belong to the children or they belong to nobody.   And if politics is the theory and practice of obtaining the ends of civil society, or the conduct of the public affairs of a State, then politics is justified by the provision it makes for the training of the coming citizens of the State.   In North Carolina the number of these future citizens is large.   Our State leads all the sisterhood of the country in its birth rate of thirty-two per thousand of population.   Utah follows.   These children are our wealth, for, as Ruskin said, there is no wealth but life.   But how shameful is the provision which we make for its husbanding and enhancement!   We stand fourth in the value of our agricultural products, forty-fourth in our provision for education.   The school term is one hundred twenty-three days against the average of one hundred sixty in the whole country.   In North Carolina six months, in New York nine months where it is not ten.   And we are 13 per cent illiterate.

To the explanation that we are eighty-one per cent rural, I charge you answer, with John Bright, that a nation lives in its cottages.   To sparse population, answer consolidate ; to sparse money, answer consolidate.   As with individuals so with communities: they can buy what they want if they agree on it and want it hard enough.

But your field of service in education is not restricted to the schools.   It extends far beyond.   Public opinion is the king of a democracy.   It needs the enlightenment of your intelligence and the drive of your conscience—in the fundamental matters of industry and thrift, personal and public health, the growing deterioration of our stock by the unrestricted mating of the obviously unfit.

I pledge you to the sovereignty of Truth, from whatsoever quarter her great eyes may look down upon you. For she comes from God and bears His message. Out of the starry deeps illimitable and radiant she comes to say, "The heavens declare the glory of God." Out of the museum of the aeons, where on stony pages aspiring life records its defeats and successes, she comes to say, "In the beginning God created the heavens and the earth, the herb yielding seed, the beast of the earth after its kind, and man in His own image." Out of far climes and dim days, thro' the blunders and tragedies and sins of history, down to the blind jeopardies of the last wild game of war, she comes to say, "The Most High ruleth in the kingdom of men and giveth it to whomsoever He will." Out of the laboratories where skilled fingers and keen eyes pick reverently a little path of light into the mystery which envelops our life, she comes to say, "The invisible things of God are clearly seen, being perceived thro' the things that are made, even His everlasting power and divinity."

And now for this last moment, dropping all trivialities of equipment, career, and task, may we not, my brothers, all join hands about the central fact to which all previous history converges, from which all subsequent history diverges with a crimson tinge forever, and at the cross of Christ challenge our central selves for our deepest interest, our highest allegiance, our souls' best love? The masters of men go by and beckon but He says, "You are mine." Epicurus with his doctrine of salvation through tranquillity and meditation calls you; the Stoics with their self-control under law; Aristotle with his restraint and proportion; Mill with his utilitarian morality; Nietzsche with his superman of ruthless might. But Christ says, "Follow me." His law of life is the law of love and renunciation. Find your life by losing it. The Cross is central in nature and in life. Redemption is there, or it is nowhere—

redemption for the individual life and for the social and national life. There is none other name given among men. As we clasp hands in parting this bright day, let us pledge anew to Him our unwavering loyalty and the full measure of our devotion. That Cross which He bore for us let us today, for good and all, take up and henceforth bear for the needy world. And may His grace and His joy be yours through all the days!

CULTURE AND TOLERATION

1923

The human scene in which you shift somewhat your positions today is various and tangled to an unexampled degree. Look about you a moment. People are very much as they have always been, but there are more of them than ever before. They are closer together. They move about faster and bump into one another oftener and more violently. Life seems to be a grand mix-up of persons, classes, nations, with boundless opportunities of coöperation, indeed, but of antagonism and collision as well. You recognize another new feature or two. The scientific view of the universe has displaced the contracted and mechanical view of the past. The applications of science have enhanced the productive capacity of the average worker, equipped human life with new apparatus, and reshaped wellnigh all the externals of civilized society. You will probably agree that the recognition of the rights of other nations is new, the spirit of internationalism which is in evidence everywhere except in Washington. But nothing is more conspicuous than the rise of the new individualism, insisting that every man counts one, now at length every woman also, thank God! Everybody rejoices in this new feature of our time. Special privilege is passed or passing. Justice is come at last. But indications of extravagance are already observed on every hand, and individualism without the restraints of Christian culture easily passes into license in personal experience and anarchy in society.

Lowering of the old standards gives every standard a chance. The decline of authority sets everybody free. One may think what one pleases and say what one thinks. And no matter how superficial or radical the view, it may count upon a following in this wild, free time. The age-long groupings are, of course, still with us. Here are conservatives and progressives in science, politics, business, and religion. The moral ideal stands over against the aesthetic ideal; the sons of Zion are still stirred up against the sons of Greece. But now there are new groupings and a new sharpness of outline in the old because of the new freedom of movement and expression. Bigotry is bold and common, bigotry in all spheres—scientific and theological, political and national, industrial, social, and professional—parties, parties, division and debate.

Such a situation cries aloud for poise and composure, for self-control and mutual respect, for discrimination of values and the subordination of irrelevant differences, for the grace of patience and the courage of a dauntless hope. I insist this is no counsel of cowardice. It involves no surrender of convictions or the watering down of truth as God gives one to see it. It is not cowardice, but generosity; not compromise, but adjustment; not surrender, but the strategy of a deferred but certain victory. I venture to think it the old word of the Master, the meek shall inherit the earth.

Where shall we look for such an attitude and influence, for such restraint and guidance? Where, if not to men who have had your opportunity of training in an institution controlled by the Christian ideal and motivated by the Christian purpose? You have learned enough to know that no man is infallible, not even yourself. I do not endorse entirely the dictum of an American university teacher when he says that only one thing is worse than that a college student should forget his subjects, and that is that he should remember them. You will forget details, but you will not forget outlines. The extent of the field of knowledge will remain with you, as also the assurance that the attitude of reverence and humility best becomes one who has caught sight of its gleaming heights and widespreading plains. . The man of culture must be tolerant. Let Philistines rage, he will be calm. Let men disagree, he will cooperate.

To be tolerant is of the nature of culture, not an acquired

habit. For culture is breadth of horizon, and breadth of horizon is made up of different points of view, and in proportion to its range and depth, multiplies the points of contact with the invisible and the unknown. Culture says there are other minds, capable, spontaneous, and genuine, reacting in individual ways to special conditions. Of course, there are divergent attitudes and views. To each mind the only view that is absolutely authentic is its own. But it cannot properly respect its own integrity and rights unless it respects the integrity and rights of others.

Culture recognizes not only the fact and legitimacy of other views, but also the limitations which beset its own. There are, for example, what may be called philosophical limitations. The mystery of pain and evil, the tragedy of sin, the universal defeat and negation of death, the ecstasy of love and beauty, the central secrets of nature, so fascinating, so elusive, forever escaping still the fine-meshed net of scientific research—who can dogmatize and dictate where so much is obscure?

Moreover, the deep things, the fundamental things, the things that matter most, defy analysis and logical treatment. They are directly apprehended in their wholeness, if at all— not discovered at the end of an argument. In the Pauline phrase, they are spiritually discerned.

> For nothing worthy proving can be proven,
> Nor yet disproven.

But so inveterate and imperious is our Western habit of reasoning out everything in heaven, on earth, and under the earth, and setting everything in its place in a logical system, that now one may find a theorem, all but a mathematical formula, for every fact—of God, of nature, of the soul, of destiny, of the eternal life, and the largest culture is in peril of confounding the formula with the fact. It is quite certain to suffer the discredit of rejecting the fact, if it is unable to manage the formula.

I warn you against the rationalism of the time which enthrones the reason as the adequate and final arbiter of all questions—the scientific rationalism which denies what it cannot handle and explain, the theological rationalism which goes beyond what is written and then seeks to enforce with anathemas subscription to the deliverances of an alien logic. But here you need to be on your guard, lest you yourself illustrate the intolerance which you disapprove. It is especially hard to be tolerant toward the intolerant. It is easier and more comforting to feel, with William Blake, that indignation is the voice of God, and to declaim and give the lash. One wishes to protect the weak against the impositions of the misinformed, to gag obscurantism speaking in the name of religion, to fetter the hand that sets up a false and injurious antithesis, as "science or religion," and scatters stones and thorns in the path of the young Greeks of our day who would see Jesus. But this is precisely the spirit of which persecution is born. And, as George Eliot said, the responsibility of tolerance lies with those who have the wider vision. We who are strong ought to bear the burdens that the weak make for themselves and us. We are not to please ourselves. Each of us must please his neighbor, doing him good by building up his faith. Fill your hands with deeds, not weapons. Speed ahead, and attacks from the rear will cease. Have faith in the spreading light. Speak the word and let it work.

With the distinct and unequivocal repudiation of any idea of sacerdotalism, permit me to suggest that you are called to discharge in a very real sense priestly functions. The priest stands for God amid the mystery and pain, the sin and sorrow, of the world. He is instinctively and utterly trusted, and shares, in a sacred confessional, with a deep and ever-hopeful compassion, the burden of broken hearts. He shares also the distress of confused and defeated minds. Recall your own experience. How eager the early inquiry! What wonders flashed in microscope and telescope and spectroscope and dynamo. Ah! that dance of the electrons, those viewless waves which travel through eternity! And looming ever and anon over all, the form of Law, somber and gigantic, cold and inexorable.

When the young explorer in this new world pauses for breath, he remembers the home, the church which seems worlds away, remembers the religious beliefs which took shape in the old restricted horizon, and finds some things incompatible with his new knowledge. He is dazed, and if no friendly, steady hand is reached out to him in this darkness and doubt, he is likely to be lost. Here is opportunity for your Christian culture and toleration. You must be priest to him then in the tender and gracious ministry of mediating the discord, of running the essentials of the old faith into the new moulds. Such a ministry requires more than the sympathizing, priestly heart. It calls for a wide intelligence in the science of the time mellowed by human interest. You must be able to go deep where separate coral islands join hands under the sea.

Another form of mediation the situation challenges you to undertake, a mediation more general in its opportunity and bearing. The truth of Christ must be mediated to a period emancipated from mere tradition by science, self-contained and independent by the growth of democracy. You must be prepared to show to business and scientific complacency that Christianity is workable, that the law of the cross lies at the heart of nature, to show to brass-tacks philosophers that the Sermon on the Mount is practical on the plain; not a distant ideal to guide our vague aspirings, but a way of life.

May I leave with you a picture and trust you to catch all its wealth of suggestion, no matter what your calling is to be? In the St. Gaudens statue of the great New England preacher the figure of Christ stands behind the figure of the preacher, and in token of sweet fellowship, of impulsion and guidance, the Master's hand is on the preacher's shoulder.

CULTURE AND FAITH

1924

I cannot say good-bye to you today and push your boat off the beach of this sheltered cove without some assurance that it is seaworthy, well-provisioned, and well-officered. There is a general apprehension of ugly weather, and the flood may bear you far. May we not counsel together these last moments of a four years' happy fellowship to make sure you are fit and trim and ready? About one thing I am particularly solicitous. If intelligence is on the prow, religion must be at the wheel. I am wondering whether you have found that the obligation to be intelligent makes it hard to be Christian. Are your culture and your faith friendly and coöperant?

It is two thousand years since the Master led a silent, wondering group of men out of the city and was parted from them on the top of Olivet. But we are in Wake Forest today because He was once on Olivet. He was the greatest of teachers and had the greatest of messages. That day he entrusted His message to His friends to expound and to spread. The succeeding generations and the expanding boundaries of human intercourse have passed that original responsibility down through the sad, slow centuries to us. And He is again in the midst of His friends—here in the midst of His friends. If we press up close about Him, we may see His lips part, His lips of strength and beauty, and hear Him say once again, "Go teach."

He wrote no book, but He was at home in the greatest of literature. He wrote no book, but He did more—He inspired the greatest of all later books. In His earthly life He was sympathetic with all the features, phases, and moods of external nature, which in His immortal life He had created by the word of His power. That attitude and interest sanctioned scientific investigation. He ministers to every section of man's nature, and proposes to control all its relationships. He is, accordingly,

[129]

concerned with all the content and environment of human life.
So must His representatives be.   One day there flashed in
splendor through His mind all the historic kingdoms of the
world while He meditated plans of His own.   He told the
official of the Roman Empire that His Kingdom was not political, or local, or material.   He was King of all those who were
open-minded to the Truth.   And this King of the truth-seekers
declared Himself to be the embodiment and illustration of the
Truth, and He who spoke the creative word of light in the
beginning said in the fullness of time, "I am the Light of the
world."

Here, in effect, the Master asserts the fellowship of religion
and learning, and imposes upon all who follow Him the obligation of the widest possible culture.   Here is the genesis of
the Christian school, its charter and program.

What was the message which Christ entrusted to His friends
and bade them proclaim out to the very fringes and borders
of humanity?   He put them in His place to continue what He
had begun.   What had He begun?

This inquiry is radical: it goes to the roots of our religion
and etches as a biting acid the outlines of our task.   It is
fundamental; it points out the foundations of the Christian
hope and achievement of all the subsequent centuries.   Once
this inquiry of the original word and purpose of Christ is
raised, superficialities become impertinent and convenient eva-
sions impossible.   We must break through a thousand professional interpreters to the Master Himself and hear His living
unamended Word, see Him at His gracious ministries.   If A
or B or C or D intervene and protest, "Who are you to ignore
the succession of the rabbis and set aside the ancient formula?"
I shall answer, "Only a lover of the Truth bent upon lighting
my taper at the Master light, only a limping follower trying to
keep in sight of Him, only a happy slave responsible to his
Master alone and not another."

The Master Himself recognized the competency of the individual when he asked, "Why even of yourselves judge ye not what is right?" And Paul complains, "Why is my liberty judged by another conscience?" James exhorts us, "So speak and so do as men that are to be judged by the law of liberty." Release from three types of slavery was signalized by the spontaneous rise of Baptists in four different countries of Europe. They came into being, as one has put it, like springs welling up from all parts of the same water-shed of history, to proclaim their release from the coercion of belief, from the coercion of ritual, and from the coercion of ecclesiastical authority. This emancipation in which our denominational forbears were born extends widely now to embrace all the Christian democracy which affirms, "One is your teacher and all you are brothers."

You must permit me to say that the time has come—fully come—to recur to the original Gospel teaching and its harmony with the widest intelligence. It is only necessary to remind you, in the first place, of a recent movement which tends to make the impression that the culture of the modern world is inherently antagonistic to the Christian faith. The movement sprang out of a genuine solicitude for the safety of our most precious possession, but it is now, particularly in the minds of the young, putting in jeopardy what it sought to preserve. It rekindles in the twentieth century the burnt-out fires of the nineteenth century controversy between religion and science, and forces again the false and injurious antithesis of the Bible or science. The spectacle is amazing and disheartening.

In the second place, I remind you of an enormous elaboration of opinion and theory hanging like a mist about the clear word of Christ. This theorizing goes beyond what is written, and like the rabbinic commentaries on the Ancient Hebrew Law, it is sometimes held to be as sacred and authoritative as the written Word. It shifts the emphasis of Christian interest from the point where Christ left it. It substitutes the dictation theory of the Scriptures for the fact of inspiration. It extends the aim of revelation to cover the facts and forces of Nature which are open to human research, and holds the phenomenal language of the Bible to strict scientific accountability. The simple New Testament pictures of the Second Coming become, in the revived Judaism of the time, an elaborate, mechanical, spectacular, political scheme, the modern counterpart of what Jesus repudiated in His day. The tragedy of Calvary, where our Lord became sin for us and laid down His life to win ours —the wonder of infinite love and the mystery of divine suffering do not protect that most hallowed spot in history against vulgar invasion, and one hears even there the clatter of logical apparatus seeking to determine how the Cross becomes efficacious, a clatter only a little less profane and alien than the gambling of the soldiers for the seamless robe.

Of course, this Christian metaphysics has its interest and uses. I seek merely to indicate its limitations. But the gentlemen of the present or the former time who have exercised their rational faculty in this human science are forever in peril of assuming for it a credit and a finality to which it has no claim. They seem inclined to set up a wholly unwarranted and mischievous issue: if you do not accept the theory, you reject the fact; if you do not approve the emendation, you deny the original; if you do not admit the conclusions of this Christian rationalism, you are a "rationalist"! If you insist that the deep things of God and the human spirit defy logical manipulation, you deny the supernatural, even in the act of asserting it!

I warn you, my brothers, against this confusion. It is responsible for much of the unhappiness of Christians and the injustice of the historic church. The darkest pages of Christian history, which we would fain never turn again, were written in this confusion. Many a man who loved Christ passionately and trusted Him in a boundless peace has been whipped out of the Christian fellowship because he could not assent to the interpretations of men no more infallible than himself, and has come not infrequently to acquiesce in the judgment and gone down to history with the stigma of infidelity attached to his name. Discriminate, my brothers, discriminate. On peril of that gravest and last disaster, the loss of your faith and the consequent shipwreck of your one life adventure, discriminate between Christ and some of His interpreters, between your personal relationship to Him and proposed explanations of it. Believe me, that personal relationship of love and loyalty to Him is the essence of the Christian experience, however it may be explained or wherever stationed in a system of religious philosophy. Trust when you cannot see. The anchor of the soul that can neither break nor drag passes in behind the veil.

But as I said at the beginning we must press through to Him, through the mist of metaphysics and the din of debate all the way up to Him for His original message. You need not hesitate. Come to Him, directly to Him. Do not be afraid. He is my friend. If you have not met Him, I should like to introduce you now. Here He is : lofty, as you see, but smiling and gracious ; the type of the manliness and beauty of our race irradiate with supernal goodness and power. Withal, how tender He is and yearning. And do you not recognize the stigmata of compassion which sought you beyond the gates of death? And He has the words of eternal life, words possessing as well as imparting eternal life. They have the gift of perpetual contemporaneousness. No matter how wide-ranging and deep-running your culture, it can never get beyond them. Nor will they ever suffer discredit in the widening horizon of modern science. They may be briefly summarized.

One of these words is that God is our Father with a genuine solicitude for His wayward children. If you would see the Father, look at Me, He says. He affirms the spirit world and presents a sample, so that commerce with it is open and easy. Another word is that the divine requirement is summarized in love. Another, that He came not to limit life, but to give life, to heighten its quality and enlarge its volume. Still another, that the law of life is the law of the Cross, and that the task of life is to proclaim the Gospel of the redemption of all life in Him and to minister to all the forms of human need, forestalling them and correcting the conditions out of which they arise. For He said, "As the Father hath sent Me, even so send I you." And this message of the teaching is illustrated and extended by the message of the sacrificial life and death.

You will see that we have here, not a system of thought, or a body of opinion, or a set of conclusions reached at the end of argument, but the challenge of the eternal world. The appeal is not to reason, but to faith, that deep-lying central capacity to see the invisible, to apprehend immediately the enveloping realm of spirit. Deep calls to deep, and if deep answers to deep, it is not because we are convinced, but because we are won.

Let this immediate apprehension of the eternal, essential things be the sun and pole-star of all your voyaging. If the fog settle, or the night, let the pilot at the wheel hear the oftener from the watchman on the prow, and hold firmly, in any case, to the course established in a happier hour of clear faith.

But

> Round the cape of a sudden comes the sea,
> And the sun looks over the mountain's rim.

Push off, and may the God of wind and wave be with every one of you in every league of your great adventure!

CULTURE AND HORIZON

1925

The Lake of Lucerne is a jewel of aquamarine in a setting of jagged Alpine heights. Mount Rigi invades its crystal depths and springs a sheer precipice through its blue-green surface. The scenery at the base of the Rigi is varied and fine, its own great outline forming the dominating feature; but at every stage of the ascent new vistas open and new beauties come into view as the horizon widens. From the crest, the lake, the plain, Tell's Chapel, may still be seen through the tinted air, but also the unimaginable one hundred twenty mile stretch of snow-crowned Alps from the Rossberg and Sentis on the east to the Jungfrau, never lifting her sweeping white veil, and somber Pilatus on the west. The climb is difficult and slow, chasms yawn for you under your upward way, and from the top you might drop disastrously into the lake four thousand feet below. But what struggles would one not endure, what perils would one not brave for such a horizon!

As in the far time of Christ, so now one must be led up an exceeding high mountain in order to see all the kingdoms of the world and the glory of them. The education of the race as of the individual is an adventure in mountain climbing. The rising levels of culture from Homer to Dante, through the spacious times of great Elizabeth to the far more spacious times in which we live, have been hard to achieve, but they have marked the successive stages of man's emancipation. Especially in the earlier periods has the advance been meager and slow, in the later it has been more rapid and sure, in the latest crowding swiftly toward its flying goal. We have been so long reaching our present point of vantage partly because knowledge is the means and condition of knowledge, partly because knowledge must wait upon the development of its apparatus, partly because the prophets of the new knowledge have always been

crucified by the scribes of the old.   But, in spite of inherent
difficulty and artificial obstruction, we are today inheritors of
the new earth of Columbus known from pole to pole and the
new heavens of Copernicus enormously expanded in the new
astronomy.   And God is not lost in the works of His hand.
All things still hold together in Christ.   Without Him we still
see that they would fly apart in unintelligible disorder.

This racial experience with lifting horizons through centuries
of discovery is epitomized in the individual experience, as the
racial development is abridged and compressed in the individual development.   Permit me to remind you of your own
first steps at the foot of the mountain of knowledge.   You were
then seeking the mastery of the tools with which you might
climb.   Then history began to unfold her ample page.   Literature introduced you to her Scott and Dickens and Hardy and
Shaw, her poets one by one, those best interpreters of man and
nature, from Longfellow to singing Tennyson, Browning ro-
bust and buoyant, rebel Ibsen throbbing with ghostly terrors,
to myriad-minded, deep-hearted Shakespeare.   Science, keen-
eyed and ardent, brought her test-tube and battery, her microscope and telescope and spectroscope, and bade you handle
with your hands, bade you see for yourself, and make your
own induction.   Some book, some lecture, some laboratory
experiment, marked the stages of your intellectual enlargement,
their exhilaration and expansion.   And today you are well up
the steep ascent.   Some profane Esau among the critics has
spoken of the total blank and vacuity of the American mind
after four years of college training.   He was probably gener-
alizing his own experience.   You have, indeed, not yet won
the summit of your Rigi.   I hope you never will, although
you keep on climbing.   Even if you are still in the olive or-
chards and chestnut groves of the lower slopes, your horizon
is wider than Galileo's, unprecedented, indeed, in all the fore-
gone time.

But no horizon is extensive unless it includes God.   In this sense horizon is another name for religion, the extension of the human horizon to include God.   Religion is the adventure of overleaping the boundaries of the physical life into the bound-less life of the spirit world.   And progress in religion is the progressive expansion of the spiritual horizon and its increasing reaction of fascination and control on the human spirit.

You need to remember, however, the peril of the heights. It is true that the plain has its peculiar perils.   There is the wrong emphasis, the exaggeration of the near view, the lack of perspective, and so we misjudge what we see.   Most serious of all is the peril of being content in our own little cabbage garden, while the illimitable universe challenges us in vain. If you respond to the challenge, a different sort of peril awaits you.   As you rise, the cold increases and the isolation, and at any point you are in peril of the last disaster of an irretrievable fall.   But these will not deter you, unless you prefer an empty and insignificant life.   In our nobler moments difficulty keys us up, and the tang of danger makes the fascination of the ad-venture.

The meaning of my little parable is manifest.   You have found the successive levels of your intellectual life hard to reach, and you have been exposed to the loss of some things which you counted precious on the lower levels.   Some col-lege students in long handling of books and apparatus have lost their love of the open spaces of field and wood, of the soil and the fair things which spring out of it.   Some have lost their old fellowships, which now seem commonplace.   And some have found it hard to keep a place in their widened hor-izon for certain cherished conceptions of their earlier expe-rience.   A young Breton priest was suddenly taken up out of the simple unperplexed religious life of the obscure province of Brittany, and transplanted into the alert and splendid life of Paris with its elaborate and gorgeous religion and the ex-panding horizon of the new knowledge.   The transition was without preparation and too abrupt, and Renan, finding the

Christianity of Brittany incompatible with the knowledge of Paris, came to count himself no longer Christian. Some college students have a similar experience. Beliefs established in the home church seem not to tally with what they learn in college. They thought, for example, that the Bible was dictated word by word to amanuenses, but find that it was written by men "inspired" of God. They thought the world and all its inhabitants were created of God in one hundred forty-four hours back in the year B. C. 4004, and discover in the science of geology the indisputable marks of an antiquity millenniums back of that date. They are confused, dazed, distressed. They first question their training in a restricted horizon and, if no friendly hand is reached out to them in this confusion, they are likely to be lost and to surrender their religious beliefs, all of them together, instead of revising some of them. Such transitions are always difficult and dangerous. The difficulty lies in making the adjustment to the new outlook, the danger in the possible loss of some of the permanent values of the past.

This sort of religious crisis is not peculiar to college students. It will be precipitated by preoccupation with intellectual or business pursuits and by any experience which gives one a new and startling view of things. The new horizon is always the judge and corrector of the old, sometimes the despoiler of the old. Just there is the point of crisis, just there the opportunity of the christian teacher, to guide sympathetically in the adjustment and revision, to mediate the discord, and, in a tender and gracious ministry, see that the essentials of the old conceptions run smoothly into the new molds. For the new knowledge will come. It is one of the aims of the process of education. The college where Christ is King is committed to the discovery and proclamation of the truth in all realms, for He declared Himself the King of the Kingdom of Truth. The Christian college will interpret history and economics and philosophy and science from the Christian point of view, and bring its children through the storm and stress, the chickenpox and measles of the intellectual life, to a large place of peace where their religion will be as secure as it is intelligent. That happy issue is sure to follow if it shows them how to distinguish between religion and proposed explanations of religion, between the religious experience and the effort to account for it in terms of intellect. You do not have to account for that inscrutable experience in the terms of any metaphysical system in order to be assured of its validity.

> Religion's all or nothing; it's no mere smile
> O' contentment, sigh of aspiration, sir—
> No quality of the finelier tempered clay
> Like its whiteness or its lightness; rather, stuff
> O' the very stuff, life of life, and self of self.

Our primary need is to be good; after that to be intelligent. I hope you have completed safely here, these four expanding years, the transition from your Brittany to your Paris, and that today your religion is at home with your culture. For religion without culture is partial, austere, inefficient, superstitious. Culture without religion is partial, unsatisfying, aimless, anarchic. But when they are combined, each in its highest development, they guarantee the happy and the victorious life.

CULTURE AND RESTRAINT

1926

A man advances in refinement as he frees himself from what is rude and gross in his thoughts, feelings, and manners, and establishes positively in his nature the control of the true, the good, and the beautiful. This sort of improvement comes mainly by the contagion of fellowship, by association with persons who have attained this inward excellence and beauty, whether walking literally by our side or giving themselves to us with less reserve in the bright pages which are the transcript of their souls. Our guides to culture are men and books, which is to say, men; for Milton taught us that a good book is the precious life-blood of a master-spirit embalmed and treasured up on purpose to a life beyond life. Accordingly, in Matthew Arnold's phrase, culture is the fruit of acquainting ourselves with the best that has been known and said in the world.

You have had here the high privilege of fellowship with men of culture. They have walked with you through the literatures of the world and the laboratories of science. They have themselves followed the history of the human spirit and marked its triumphs. They have led you along that brightening path. They have themselves pressed resolutely into the mystery which envelops us on every hand, and they have asked you to share with them that holy adventure. They have themselves seen the radiant and ordered beauty of our Father's house of many mansions, from whirling electrons to the universe of stars, from bacterium to man; and these four years, with a secret joy I have watched them showing you about the place, like the interpreter in the old allegory. And you—I have seen you shy and awkward, gaining by degrees confidence and ease of manner; I have seen that subtle sculptor, intelligence, rechiseling your countenance, your vagrant interests settling to a consistent purpose, ideals organizing themselves in character, dreams becoming policies, your intellectual horizon widening, your attitude softening into catholicity; in short, boys growing into men, alert and thoughtful, self-controlled and at home in the world of men and things.

This is culture in process and result. It authenticates itself by what you are, not by what you have; by the way you feel, not by what you know; by the fellowships of your spirit, not by the work of your hands. It is inward wealth which accountants cannot inventory, which time, the pilferer, cannot reach. The secret of your power in mid career is there. And in after years when fortune still waits below the horizon, when friends fall away, when outside activities and interests steadily contract with the inevitableness of fate, these inner resources will guarantee your independence and refresh you as fountains in waste places.

But I call your mind to the other side of this shield. I name it restraint. For restraint is of a piece with culture; it is only another aspect of culture. It is compounded of moderation, reverence, and humility. Of moderation. There is neither culture nor virtue in excess. Poise and balance and respect for the integrity and insight of others result from a just view all round. Propagandists have little interest in the truth itself. The inferiority complex of the psychoanalysts throws light on the ardor of many extremists. We always become fanatical when we are afraid of facts which we dare not face, and it is easy to be intolerant and abusive. A genuine culture, not to say the Christian spirit, restrains such extravagance.

Irreverence is the advertisement of a defective culture. You will allow me to say that this voyage of discovery in far lands, a stage of which you complete today, has meant little to you, if it has not deepened your awe in the presence of the majesty of the sum of things. The deep vision of the microscope, the long vision of the telescope, those radiations which flash and dance in the vacuum-tube and frolic through seven feet of lead,

the progressive achievements of organic life following the beck-
oning hand of God, the psychic inheritance of the race with
its tragedies and triumphs, which has flowed down on you,
the universe of spirit, invisible but real, which envelops all
and penetrates all—I despair of you, my brothers, if in such a
contemplation your spirits do not bow in reverence for what
is beneath you, for what is around you, for what is within you,
and for what is above you.

Rich and varied and wide-ranging as our culture is, it has
its limitations, and these will dispose us to humility. For all
the harvest of the new knowledge, for all our lately acquired
control of the forces of nature and the limitless expansion of
the universe in space and time, for all our new imaginative
conceptions and our revised intellectual and moral attitudes,
we have discovered that we have been occupied with the surface of things, not their inner meaning, with what goes on before our eyes, not the linking up of things, not their drive or
direction. The problems which we have solved have only introduced us to new and deeper problems, and it now appears
that the more we know, the less we know. In physics and
chemistry and biology at every crucial point men say, "I do
not know, I do not know." Science seems to be declining
into nescience. And consider the field of personality now at
length included in the natural realm. The physical principles
and tests which break down at the interesting point in the investigation of things are even more disappointing when applied to thoughts, memory, emotion, faith, which constitute
personality. Plato and St. Francis and Shakespeare and Lee
have clearly a place in the natural order, and if science cannot explain them, one might ask if it has explained anything.
The very conceptual apparatus for "explaining" the phenomena of personality remains to be invented. Ether and electron
and ion are clearly inapplicable. There is no algebra of love.
The attraction which draws two souls together does not vary
inversely as the square of the distance. Accordingly, the cru-

cial questions in all fields of inquiry are questions still.   The
great scientists—there are minor scientists as there are minor
poets—admit their limitations and agree that there are spheres
of reality to which their methods and instruments are inappro-
priate.

Permit me to press yet another fact which pricks the balloon
of our conceit and reduces the most highly privileged of us to
teachableness and humility.   Consider how the body of knowledge itself seems to be falling to pieces.   Not a little of the
science of thirty years ago the science of today appears to have
discredited.   Things have been smashed to atoms including
the atom.   The "elements" are composite and transmutable.
The straight line is curved.   The conservation of energy does
not conserve.   The stately law of gravitation shows signs of
an unseemly levity.   At a recent scientific meeting a paper was
read on the subject, "The Vacuum : there is Something in It."
What Huxley considered the most fundamental and universal
antithesis in nature, matter and force, no longer exists.   When
a man was asked what was the difference between cherubim
and seraphim, he replied that there used to be a difference
between them, but they had made it up.   Matter and force
have compounded their differences and merged in electricity.
What is a plain man to think?   Is science a modern Saturn
devouring its own children?   Has science kicked its own bottom out, or only opened deeper abysses of mystery?   In any
case, we now know that we do not know as much as we thought
we knew.   We have been accumulating ignorance rapidly of
late.

But come to think of it, the discovery of a mistake is not
ignorance, however wholesome a restraint it may prove upon
our pride.   It is discovery, an item of new knowledge.   The
moment between the discovery of a mistake and its correction
may be a moment of darkness, but it is a prophecy of light.
Such moments in the progress of science have been scored
against it as a reproach and a demonstration of its unreliability.

A book in biology or physics ten years old is out of date, it is said, and today's authoritative deliverance is likely to be changed tomorrow. But this attitude of devotion to truth, not to past formulations of truth, is precisely the ground of confidence in science. Some men like the cozy comfort of traditions securely barred against the chill and disorder of invasion from without. Give me the open windows and the fresh airs blowing in from everywhere. For God is in His world, in every quarter of it, and there can be nothing so excellent or so commanding as to have Him blow in on our smug conceit with a new revelation in the light of which our garnered knowledge looks like ignorance.

And yet, with all this wholesome chastening of spirit, your culture puts you at home in the world of men and things. How about the people to whom you return? They have not had your opportunity; will they have your attitude? If you offend them by superior airs, you discredit your culture. If you ignore them, you deny it. If you have learned well your limitations, you will sympathize with theirs. For it must be admitted that many of us are engrossed with transient and superficial matters and choose inferior pleasures and pursuits. Some are contemptuous of culture and announce their indifference to the higher forms of art in letters, in painting, in music, without perceiving that they compromise themselves. In the particular field of science there is an appalling lack of information. Though science touches life at well-nigh all points, it appears to have made in wide areas no impression, except to awaken resistance. Witness the survival of superstition in the minds of socalled educated people. Witness the widespread obscurantism which identifies the new learning with heresy. Witness the heated controversies in certain religious circles about irrelevant matters long ago settled by responsible men of science. Witness the determination of public issues in local and national legislatures by personal and partisan considerations with no notion of the scientific method of investigation, with no knowledge of the discoveries of science bearing upon those issues. And what shall we think of our complacent and bumptious provincialism in an era of intercourse? of the Bostonian who thinks nothing ever happened west of the Hudson River? of the Minnesotan who refuses to allow his daughter to follow her husband to a Southern college professorship, because society "way down South" is rude and dangerous? And here is the Senate of the United States, with Mexico and Russia and Afghanistan, aloof from the organized intelligence and conscience of mankind, insisting with the vision of a blind kitten that the sun is not yet up, that the international barriers long ago transformed by science into means of communication are barriers still, ordained of God and George Washington, and maintaining that the cooperation of independent nations against the crime of war and for the promotion of their common interests is a compromise of their sovereignty, rather than an assertion of it.

Here is the tragedy of the segregation of learning. And your obligation is manifest. This gap between the school and the people, the college and the people, must be closed. The college has extension courses, but nothing is so effective as this sifting out into the general citizenship of men of your attainments and standards, men of culture and restraint. You are called to diffuse intelligence, to protect the weak against the impositions of the uninformed. A particular service demanded of you just at this time is to disabuse people's minds of the idea that science is the enemy of religion. The universe is rational, or science is impossible. It is beautiful—have you not seen a section of it? It is beneficent, for God said in the beginning that it was good. And the study of it with such gifts and apparatus as we have is noble and wholesome. So also we must insist that the universe of spirit is but the extension of the upper plane of reality.

Manifestly science cannot discredit faith. The deeper things of nature and life are beyond its plummet. Materialism has

10

lost what scientific support it once had. The scientist today is the fool of Scripture when he denies God and the spirit world. Almost unanimously men of science are taking the opposite attitude. They are feeling that a system of things out of which mind arose must itself be mental at bottom; that the order of the universe suggests an Infinite Intelligence, its beauty an Infinite Artist, its invisible ministries an Infinite Friend. They have done little beyond presenting examples of the miraculous, lifting the curtain on wonder. And we have to thank them for a greater universe and a greater God. With a clearer and ampler radiance the heavens declare the glory of God, and the solid firmament of the Psalmist, dissolved now into the expanse of the illimitable universe of stars, shows the Divine Handiwork with new and overwhelming impressiveness. And so I think of science as walking to and fro in God's garden, busying itself with its forms of beauty, its fruits and flowers, its beast and bird and creeping thing, the crystals shut in its stones and the gold grains of its sands, and coming now at length in the cool of the long day upon God Himself walking in His garden.

CULTURE AND LIFE

1927

On Wednesday night you were good and patient enough to hear extended remarks pertinent to your graduation from this institution. I would fain spare you a further draft upon your generosity, but I am not free. I am the victim of a tradition of the elders which I dare not violate. Moreover, the very form in which I observe the precedent is set for me. For many years the addresses to your predecessors have dealt with culture in relation to some phase of the intellectual life of the moment, as "Democracy" in 1910, "Patriotism" in 1916, "Crisis" in 1918, "Internationalism" in 1921, "Toleration" in 1924, "Restraint" in 1926. I am today under the tyranny of my own habit. Accordingly, as I conclude the series, I speak to you briefly on "Culture and Life." All the specific matters heretofore presented are but phases of life, which comprehends all and summarizes all.

Some one has defined culture as the harmonious expansion of all the powers which make the beauty and worth of human nature. It is a sort of beneficent infection which you catch out of the atmosphere of the Best, the best things, the best men. Here for four years you have been in such an atmosphere. You have been occupied with things of physical nature and with things of the spirit of man. The habits of mind which we associate with scientific studies are the gift of seeing things straight and telling of them truly, expectancy with its door opening eastward—Whitman thought of his heart as an inn with 100 doors all open—caution, independence, freedom, tolerance. The habits of mind which we connect with liberal studies are, in Gilbert Murray's fine phrases, the philosophic temper, the gentle judgment, the interest in knowledge and beauty for their own sake.

These gifts and graces are so many excellences of the human

nature. They at once adorn it and proclaim its worth. I have called them habits of mind, you observe; not stores. They are powers and attitudes, the way of looking at things, of feeling about things, with little or nothing to do with loads of information, which may be dropped more easily than taken on. In other words, your studies here have not filled you up with something, but improved your quality, widened the range of your interests and fellowships, made you citizens in the republic of the mind. You do not need to be reminded that these processes of culture are not completed. They never are. Diplomas merely mean that you are started in this endless self-cultivation, I hope well started. It will go forward as you meet fine men and women in high station or in low, of this race or that, as you attach yourself to noble causes, as you pasture in the fields of literature and art, and as you give your soul a chance to stretch her wings in the clear air of aspiration and communion.

Such expansion and refinement of nature will express itself in the careers which you shortly begin, but especially in the use which you make of your leisure. We have been at fault in thinking too exclusively of education as preparation for our work, for a successful career, for earning money or position more easily and more certainly. The etymology of the word *school* might have saved us from that improper emphasis. It comes to us from the Greek word *schole*, which means spare time or leisure.

Preparation for a career is a sort of apprenticeship wherein we learn to use the tools of our calling, and it may have but slight influence upon the apprentices themselves. A small man may make big money. Not a few men in the professions achieve success and remain boors. If a man's life consists not in the abundance of the things which he possesses, it may well be questioned whether our work is more important than our leisure. It is certainly true that a man will show what he is by the way he occupies himself outside his office. Culture is for leisure, that is, for life itself. And Ruskin will tell you there is no wealth but life.

Tried by this test, American life falls short. Matthew Arnold considered that we had handled our political problem well, that we had made good progress in our industrial organization, but that, with all the dazzling efficiency of our civilization, it remained uninteresting, lacking elevation and beauty. We do our work well, but we lead meager lives. We are progressive in the machinery of life, but backward in the elements which go to build up a complete human life. Many years ago our own Lowell said that we were the most common-schooled and the least cultivated of the Western nations. Does not the indictment still hold? We are tyrannized by superstition. We are intolerant. We are easy victims of the demagogue and the propagandist. Boredom is said to be the American malady, which is to say that we are destitute within, having scant inward resources and a narrow range of interests. We have not yet attained strikingly and widely the finest flower and fruit of the American spirit, a genuine culture. And now that science is emancipating us from absorption in meeting our primary needs and so increasing the proportion of our leisure, the opportunity and obligation are all the more insistent to enrich and expand our life for its higher satisfaction and uses.

I charge you, build yourself up on the inside. In whatever calling you spend your days, you will be a man first and a preacher, lawyer, doctor, teacher, banker afterwards—a man who is preaching or teaching or doctoring. The quality of the man will, of course, affect profoundly the quality of your work. But, as the man is more than the calling, so his life overflows into extra-professional channels where he may do his best service as citizen, churchman, father, and at the same time find the main currents of his personal happiness. What you want, therefore, is more *man*, a life which the white-haired poet of Camden describes as copious, vehement, spiritual, bold.

I should be untrue to you and to myself in this last opportunity if I omitted to give you the secret of this complete and radiant manhood. I have read in Paul its standard—"the measure of the stature of the fulness of Christ." And the Master Himself said, "I came that they may have life and may have it abundantly." It is He who enlarges the volume and enhances the quality of life. He is the secret of that harmonious expansion of our powers which we have called culture. You will not find the highest culture apart from Him. Sweep the universe with telescope and microscope. Range backward through all the corridors of history. Drink at all the fountains of learning, and drink deeply. Walk with Phidias and Angelo and Rembrandt in all the high places where Beauty holds her court. Attend when Beethoven and Wagner strike all the singing chords in the soul of man. Even so, without Christ your culture will want consistency and elevation; it will be empty and aimless and cold. He will transform and ennoble and beautify you in the inward parts, if you give yourself to Him without evasion or reserve, and in all coming days, bright days and dark days, you will find His joy to be your joy and your strength.

Feb. 4. 1939